W0010743

# ACT Aspire
## SUCCESS STRATEGIES
## Grade 4
## Math/Science

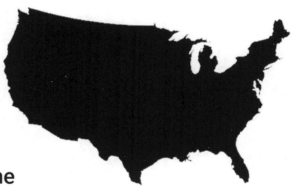

ACT Aspire Test Review for the
ACT Aspire Assessments

ISBN: 978-1-5167-0034-9

# DEAR FUTURE EXAM SUCCESS STORY

First of all, **THANK YOU** for purchasing Mometrix study materials!

Second, congratulations! You are one of the few determined test-takers who are committed to doing whatever it takes to excel on your exam. **You have come to the right place.** We developed these study materials with one goal in mind: to deliver you the information you need in a format that's concise and easy to use.

In addition to optimizing your guide for the content of the test, we've outlined our recommended steps for breaking down the preparation process into small, attainable goals so you can make sure you stay on track.

We've also analyzed the entire test-taking process, identifying the most common pitfalls and showing how you can overcome them and be ready for any curveball the test throws you.

Standardized testing is one of the biggest obstacles on your road to success, which only increases the importance of doing well in the high-pressure, high-stakes environment of test day. Your results on this test could have a significant impact on your future, and this guide provides the information and practical advice to help you achieve your full potential on test day.

### Your success is our success

**We would love to hear from you!** If you would like to share the story of your exam success or if you have any questions or comments in regard to our products, please contact us at **800-673-8175** or **support@mometrix.com**.

Thanks again for your business and we wish you continued success!

Sincerely,
The Mometrix Test Preparation Team

Copyright © 2021 by Mometrix Media LLC. All rights reserved.
Written and edited by the Mometrix Test Preparation Team
Printed in the United States of America

# TABLE OF CONTENTS

# Mathematics

PLACE VALUE AND NUMBER SENSE

LESSON 1

PLACE VALUE BIG NUMBERS 1-1,000,000

The place value of a digit is determined by where it is in a number.

| Millions | Hundred Thousands | Ten Thousands | Thousands | Hundreds | Tens | Ones |
|----------|-------------------|---------------|-----------|----------|------|------|
| 1 | 2 | 3 | 4 | 5 | 6 | 7 |

1,234,567

One million, two hundred thirty-four thousand, five hundred sixty-seven

1.  6,138,462 =

| 6 | 1 | 3 | 8 | 4 | 6 | 2 |
|---|---|---|---|---|---|---|
| Millions | Hundred Thousands | Ten Thousands | Thousands | Hundreds | Tens | Ones |

2.  3,194,675 =

| | | | | | | |
|---|---|---|---|---|---|---|
| Millions | Hundred Thousands | Ten Thousands | Thousands | Hundreds | Tens | Ones |

3.  8,417,205 =

| | | | | | | |
|---|---|---|---|---|---|---|
| Millions | Hundred Thousands | Ten Thousands | Thousands | Hundreds | Tens | Ones |

4.  2,765,447 =

| | | | | | | |
|---|---|---|---|---|---|---|
| Millions | Hundred Thousands | Ten Thousands | Thousands | Hundreds | Tens | Ones |

5.  5,925,057 =

| | | | | | | |
|---|---|---|---|---|---|---|
| Millions | Hundred Thousands | Ten Thousands | Thousands | Hundreds | Tens | Ones |

Copyright © Mometrix Media. You have been licensed one copy of this document for personal use only. Any other reproduction or redistribution is strictly prohibited. All rights reserved.

## LESSON 2

### IDENTIFYING PLACE VALUE - WORD PROBLEMS

**Solve the word problems below.**

1. In the number 25,483 :
   A. This digit is in the ones place _____
   B. This digit is in the hundreds place _____
   C. The 5 is in the _____ place
   D. The 8 is in the _____ place

2. In the number 62,134 :
   A. This digit is in the tens place _____
   B. This digit is in the thousands place _____
   C. The 6 is in the _____ place
   D. The 4 is in the _____ place

3. In the number 84,327 :
   A. This digit is in the ones place _____
   B. This digit is in the thousands place _____
   C. The 2 is in the _____ place
   D. The 8 is in the _____ place

4. In the number 14,960 :
   A. This digit is in the hundreds place _____
   B. This digit is in the ten-thousands place _____
   C. The 0 is in the _____ place
   D. The 4 is in the _____ place

5. In the number 40,589 :
   A. This digit is in the ones place _____
   B. This digit is in the hundreds place _____
   C. The 0 is in the _____ place
   D. The 4 is in the _____ place

Copyright © Mometrix Media. You have been licensed one copy of this document for personal use only. Any other reproduction or redistribution is strictly prohibited. All rights reserved.

## LESSON 3

### ROUNDING UP TO 100,000

**Round the following numbers to the nearest thousand.**

| | | | | |
|---|---|---|---|---|
| **1.** | 2,563 _____ | | **6.** | 4,219 _____ |
| **2.** | 9,198 _____ | | **7.** | 5,756 _____ |
| **3.** | 1,423 _____ | | **8.** | 8,154 _____ |
| **4.** | 7,712 _____ | | **9.** | 6,069 _____ |
| **5.** | 3,300 _____ | | **10** | 1,995 _____ |

**Round the following numbers to the nearest ten-thousand.**

| | | | | |
|---|---|---|---|---|
| **11.** | 39,092 _____ | | **16.** | 77,150 _____ |
| **12.** | 19,917 _____ | | **17.** | 33,809 _____ |
| **13.** | 93,254 _____ | | **18.** | 35,451 _____ |
| **14.** | 56,055 _____ | | **19.** | 20,901 _____ |
| **15.** | 70,856 _____ | | **20.** | 48,599 _____ |

**Round the following numbers to the nearest hundred-thousand.**

| | | | | |
|---|---|---|---|---|
| **21.** | 274,333 _____ | | **26.** | 317,110 _____ |
| **22.** | 596,559 _____ | | **27.** | 882,658 _____ |
| **23.** | 221,324 _____ | | **28.** | 610,567 _____ |
| **24.** | 530,708 _____ | | **29.** | 789,381 _____ |
| **25.** | 189,365 _____ | | **30.** | 109,277 _____ |

Copyright © Mometrix Media. You have been licensed one copy of this document for personal use only. Any other reproduction or redistribution is strictly prohibited. All rights reserved.

## LESSON 4

### EXPANDED FORM

We learned earlier that every digit in a number has a place value.
**Expanded form** shows that number expanded into an addition statement.

**Example:**

The expanded form of 5,786 is:
5,000 + 700 + 80 + 6.

## Write each number in expanded form.

1.   82    **2.**   29    **3.**   56    **4.**   74

    80 + 2    _____    _____    _____

5.   35    **6.**   99    **7.**   250   **8.**   629

    _____    _____    _____    _____

9.   150   **10.**  892   **11.**  905   **12.**  427

    _____    _____    _____    _____

**13.** Twenty - Nine    **14.** Seventy - One    **15.** Eighty - Six

    20 + 9    _____    _____

**16.** Fifty - Four    **17.** Sixteen    **18.** Thirty - Eight

    _____    _____    _____

4

Copyright © Mometrix Media. You have been licensed one copy of this document for personal use only. Any other reproduction or redistribution is strictly prohibited. All rights reserved.

## LESSON 5

### ORDERING UP TO 10,000

Write these numbers in order from least to greatest.

1. 9,289 | 92,891 | 9,281 | 96,381    9,281  9,289  92,891  96,381

2. 23,112 | 23,111 | 22,311 | 2,313 _____

3. 7,856 | 7,855 | 78,855 | 78,856 _____

4. 11,112 | 1,111 | 11,131 | 10,112 _____

5. 4,326 | 44,326 | 44,436 | 4,316 _____

6. 3,289 | 3,891 | 3,819 | 3,818 _____

7. 57,289 | 57,891 | 57,211 | 57,500 _____

8. 60,255 | 6,552 | 66,252 | 6,255 _____

9. 15,247 | 15,250 | 15,248 | 15,249 _____

10. 9,564 | 92,564 | 9,546 | 93,564 _____

11. 8,219 | 84,921 | 84,218 | 84,219 _____

Copyright © Mometrix Media. You have been licensed one copy of this document for personal use only. Any other reproduction or redistribution is strictly prohibited. All rights reserved.

**ORDERING UP TO 100,000**

Write these numbers in order from least to greatest.

1.  100,289 | 100,891 | 100,280 | 100,381 _____

2.  512,112 | 512,123 | 51,110 | 512,101 _____

3.  855,622 | 865,622 | 856,628 | 856,629 _____

4.  634,209 | 634,101 | 635,700 | 633,601 _____

5.  231,115 | 20,115 | 231,150 | 21,115 _____

6.  546,029 | 546,209 | 546,030 | 546,020 _____

7.  375,787 | 355,891 | 355,111 | 375,375 _____

8.  23,151 | 239,151 | 237,151 | 240,151 _____

9.  155,289 | 146,891 | 145,280 | 145,381 _____

10. 269,722 | 20,722 | 269,772 | 266,722 _____

11. 990,281 | 90,821 | 90,280 | 90,281 _____

12. 175,337 | 76,337 | 75,337 | 7,537 _____

Copyright © Mometrix Media. You have been licensed one copy of this document for personal use only. Any other reproduction or redistribution is strictly prohibited. All rights reserved.

# LESSON 6

## NUMBER PATTERNS TO 10,000

**Complete the number patterns.**

1.  10,475 | 10,485 | __10,495__ | __11,005__

2.  98,211 | _____ | _____ | 98,511

3.  _____ | 62,001 | _____ | 64,001

4.  22,729 | 22,829 | _____ | _____

5.  _____ | 82,657 | _____ | 84,657

6.  2,475 | 2,485 | _____ | _____

7.  11,303 | _____ | _____ | 14,303

8.  _____ | 42,370 | _____ | 44,370

9.  72,112 | 72,119 | _____ | _____

10. 33,776 | _____ | _____ | 36,776

12. _____ | 79,061 | _____ | 99,061

7

Copyright © Mometrix Media. You have been licensed one copy of this document for personal use only. Any other reproduction or redistribution is strictly prohibited. All rights reserved.

## NUMBER PATTERNS TO 100,000

### Complete the number patterns.

1.  980,211 | _____ | _____ | 980,511

2.  _____ | 621,001 | _____ | 619,001

3.  282,729 | 282,829 | _____ | _____

4.  _____ | 694,657 | _____ | 694,677

5.  111,729 | 112,729 | _____ | _____

6.  _____ | 350,001 | _____ | 352,001

7.  523,303 | _____ | _____ | 526,303

8.  _____ | 815,370 | _____ | 825,370

9.  _____ | 256,119 | 356,119 | _____

10. 609,776 | _____ | _____ | 639,776

11. 110,383 | 115,383 | _____ | _____

12. 340,303 | _____ | _____ | 370,303

Copyright © Mometrix Media. You have been licensed one copy of this document for personal use only. Any other reproduction or redistribution is strictly prohibited. All rights reserved.

## CHAPTER 2 - ADDITION

## LESSON 1

## 2-DIGIT ADDITION - REGROUPING

To add multiple digit numbers together, start in the ones place and then use basic addition rules. When the number equals ten or more the first digit carries over to the next spot. This is called **regrouping**.

| | Hundreds | Tens | Ones |
|---|---|---|---|
| **Step 1:** Add the digits in the ones column. | | 8 | 5 |
| | + 1 | 7 |
| | | | 2 |

| | Hundreds | Tens | Ones |
|---|---|---|---|
| **Step 2:** Carry the 1 over to the top of the tens column. | | 1 | |
| | | 8 | 5 |
| | x | 1 | 7 |
| | | ① | 2 |

| | Hundreds | Tens | Ones |
|---|---|---|---|
| **Step 3:** Add all the digits in the tens column together. | | 1 | |
| | | 8 | 5 |
| | x | + 1 | 7 |
| | 1 | 0 | 2 |

## Solve the problems below.

| 1. | 49<br>+ 3 2<br>‾‾‾‾‾<br>8 1 | 2. | 5 8<br>+  7<br>‾‾‾‾‾ | 3. | 8 3<br>+ 8 4<br>‾‾‾‾‾ | 4. | 4 2<br>+  9<br>‾‾‾‾‾ | 5. | 5 2<br>+ 7 2<br>‾‾‾‾‾ |
|---|---|---|---|---|---|---|---|---|---|

| 6. | 4 4<br>+  5<br>‾‾‾‾‾ | 7. | 3 2<br>+ 1 4<br>‾‾‾‾‾ | 8. | 1 8<br>+ 2 0<br>‾‾‾‾‾ | 9. | 7 1<br>+ 9 2<br>‾‾‾‾‾ | 10. | 5 9<br>+  6<br>‾‾‾‾‾ |
|---|---|---|---|---|---|---|---|---|---|

| 11. | 8 1<br>+  9<br>‾‾‾‾‾ | 12. | 6 0<br>+ 5 7<br>‾‾‾‾‾ | 13. | 3 2<br>+ 4 0<br>‾‾‾‾‾ | 14. | 1 9<br>+  2<br>‾‾‾‾‾ | 15. | 2 7<br>+ 8 6<br>‾‾‾‾‾ |
|---|---|---|---|---|---|---|---|---|---|

Copyright © Mometrix Media. You have been licensed one copy of this document for personal use only. Any other reproduction or redistribution is strictly prohibited. All rights reserved.

## LESSON 2

## 2-DIGIT 3-ROW ADDITION - REGROUPING

To add multiple digit numbers together, start in the ones place and then use basic addition rules. When the number equals ten or more the first digit carries over to the next spot. This is called **regrouping**.

**Solve the problems below.**

| 1. | 36 | 2. | 84 | 3. | 64 | 4. | 57 | 5. | 44 |
|----|----|----|----|----|----|----|----|----|----|
| | 22 | | 70 | | 29 | | 52 | | 15 |
| | + 15 | | + 9 | | + 42 | | + 73 | | + 39 |

| 6. | 66 | 7. | 50 | 8. | 15 | 9. | 67 | 10. | 11 |
|----|----|----|----|----|----|----|----|----|----|
| | 99 | | 36 | | 35 | | 72 | | 28 |
| | + 82 | | + 55 | | + 80 | | + 18 | | + 37 |

| 11. | 62 | 12. | 55 | 13. | 18 | 14. | 22 | 15. | 77 |
|-----|----|-----|----|-----|----|-----|----|-----|----|
| | 97 | | 20 | | 19 | | 76 | | 37 |
| | + 19 | | + 12 | | + 20 | | + 8 | | + 47 |

| 16. | 46 | 17. | 98 | 18. | 75 | 19. | 36 | 20. | 99 |
|-----|----|-----|----|-----|----|-----|----|-----|----|
| | 44 | | 49 | | 57 | | 62 | | 95 |
| | + 56 | | + 89 | | + 6 | | + 19 | | + 92 |

Copyright © Mometrix Media. You have been licensed one copy of this document for personal use only. Any other reproduction or redistribution is strictly prohibited. All rights reserved.

## LESSON 3

## ADDITION WORD PROBLEMS

### Use addition to solve the problems below.

1. Elle picked apples for four days. On day one she picked 10 apples. On day two she picked 26 apples. On day three she picked 14 apples. On day four she picked 14 apples. How many apples does Elle have in total?

_____

2. Cindy has been doing her chores every day after school. On Monday she swept the floor for 12 minutes. On Tuesday she spent 9 minutes making her bed. On Wednesday she washed the dishes for 20 minutes. On Thursday she spent 15 minutes vacuuming the floor. How much time did she spend on her chores?

_____

3. Steven is good at basketball. In game one he scored 14 points. In game two he scored 22 points. In game three he scored 27. In games four and five he scored 17 and 12 points. How many points has Steven scored so far?

_____

4. Amy loves to read. She reads every day after school. One day she read 45 minutes. The next day she read 30 minutes. The day after that she spent 57 minutes reading. Yesterday she read for 26 minutes and today she spent 15 minutes reading her book. How much time has she spent reading this week?

_____

Copyright © Mometrix Media. You have been licensed one copy of this document for personal use only. Any other reproduction or redistribution is strictly prohibited. All rights reserved.

## LESSON 4

## 3-DIGIT ADDITION - REGROUPING

To add multiple-digit numbers together, start in the ones place
and then use basic addition rules. When a number equals
ten or more the first digit carries over to the next spot.
This is called **regrouping**.

| Step 1:<br>Add the digits in<br>the one's column<br>and carry over the<br>1 to the ten's column. | Step 2:<br>Next add the digits in the<br>tens's column and carry<br>over the 1 to the<br>hundred's column. | Step 3:<br>Next add the digits in the<br>hundred's column. | Step 4:<br>Finally, carry over the 1<br>from the hundred's column<br>to the thousands's column. |
|---|---|---|---|

| 1000's | 100's | 10's | 1's |
|---|---|---|---|
|  |  | 1 |  |
|  | 6 | 4 | 3 |
| + | 5 | 8 | 9 |
|  |  |  | 2 |

| 1000's | 100's | 10's | 1's |
|---|---|---|---|
|  | 1 | 1 |  |
|  | 6 | 4 | 3 |
| + | 5 | 8 | 9 |
|  |  | 3 | 2 |

| 1000's | 100's | 10's | 1's |
|---|---|---|---|
|  | 1 | 1 |  |
|  | 6 | 4 | 3 |
| + | 5 | 8 | 9 |
|  | 2 | 3 | 2 |

| 1000's | 100's | 10's | 1's |
|---|---|---|---|
|  | 1 | 1 |  |
|  | 6 | 4 | 3 |
| + | 5 | 8 | 9 |
| 1 | 2 | 3 | 2 |

### Solve the problems below. Use regrouping when needed.

1.  498
   +321
   ─────
    819

2.  580
   +729

3.  134
   + 22

4.  309
   +447

5.  253
   +203

6.  171
   + 82

7.  344
   +493

8.  714
   +507

9.  629
   + 78

10. 629
   +351

Copyright © Mometrix Media. You have been licensed one copy of this document for personal use only. Any other reproduction or redistribution is strictly prohibited. All rights reserved.

## LESSON 5

### 3-DIGIT 3-ROW ADDITION - REGROUPING

To add multiple digit numbers together, start in the ones place and then use basic addition rules. When the number equals ten or more the first digit carries over to the next spot. This is called **regrouping**.

**Solve the problems below using regrouping.**

| | | | | |
|---|---|---|---|---|
| 1. 209 158 +472 ___ 839 | 2. 456 41 +137 | 3. 652 189 +305 | 4. 572 267 +453 | 5. 711 209 +374 |
| 6. 455 126 +907 | 7. 501 472 +904 | 8. 782 106 +313 | 9. 955 572 +117 | 10. 389 411 +354 |
| 11. 111 684 +243 | 12. 254 906 +145 | 13. 715 355 +742 | 14. 742 279 +109 | 15. 958 144 +302 |
| 16. 621 435 +905 | 17. 322 532 +814 | 18. 752 962 +103 | 19. 884 222 +606 | 20. 308 144 +722 |

Copyright © Mometrix Media. You have been licensed one copy of this document for personal use only. Any other reproduction or redistribution is strictly prohibited. All rights reserved.

## LESSON 6

## 4-DIGIT ADDITION - REGROUPING

Solve the problems below using regrouping.

1.  6 8 9 5
   + 5 4 0 6
   ─────────
    1 2 3 0 1

2.  1 2 5 9
   + 9 5 0 2

3.  9 5 4 3
   + 7 8 4 5

4.  4 0 5 1
   + 1 1 5 0

5.  8 5 0 7
   + 9 8 4 7

6.  3 2 5 0
   +   4 0 6

7.  2 4 7 0
   + 3 3 5 7

8.  1 5 8 9
   + 6 8 7 5

9.  5 5 7 9
   + 6 0 7 7

10.  1 0 8 9
    + 2 7 8 6

11.  7 7 5 0
    +   5 9 7

12.  3 3 7 8
    + 4 5 0 8

13.  6 9 1 7
    + 7 5 0 2

14.  4 3 2 9
    +   9 9 9

15.  9 9 4 8
    +   1 1 3

16.  4 7 0 5
    + 4 8 6 6

17.  1 5 8 0
    + 3 9 8 7

18.  2 7 7 8
    + 4 8 9 1

19.  5 5 7 6
    +   5 6 9

20.  3 5 2 0
    + 1 3 3 9

Copyright © Mometrix Media. You have been licensed one copy of this document for personal use only. Any other reproduction or redistribution is strictly prohibited. All rights reserved.

## LESSON 7

## 4-DIGIT 3-ROW ADDITION - REGROUPING

Solve the problems below using regrouping.

**1.**  1 0 9 1
  2 1 5 7
+ 3 2 6 7
‾‾‾‾‾‾‾‾
  6 5 1 5

**2.**  9 8 1 5
  4 8 0 3
+ 2 2 1 6
‾‾‾‾‾‾‾‾

**3.**  3 8 9 1
  1 2 5 9
+ 7 5 2 0
‾‾‾‾‾‾‾‾

**4.**  2 5 5 2
  8 4 0 6
+ 2 2 7 1
‾‾‾‾‾‾‾‾

**5.**  5 3 3 0
  1 2 1 1
+ 9 8 0 1
‾‾‾‾‾‾‾‾

**6.**  4 8 8 1
  2 0 0 9
+ 1 9 8 7
‾‾‾‾‾‾‾‾

**7.**  3 0 7 2
  1 6 5 0
+ 1 5 7 8
‾‾‾‾‾‾‾‾

**8.**  1 9 8 5
  8 1 0 5
+ 1 7 7 6
‾‾‾‾‾‾‾‾

**9.**  9 8 4 1
  2 7 5 0
+ 1 3 4 9
‾‾‾‾‾‾‾‾

**10.**  5 4 0 0
  7 5 0 1
+ 3 8 1 4
‾‾‾‾‾‾‾‾

**11.**  7 0 7 2
  6 1 5 2
+ 1 7 8 5
‾‾‾‾‾‾‾‾

**12.**  1 7 0 7
  1 8 0 4
+ 2 9 5 0
‾‾‾‾‾‾‾‾

**13.**  2 4 0 0
  3 9 6 2
+ 8 8 1 5
‾‾‾‾‾‾‾‾

**14.**  6 0 7 4
  1 2 5 5
+ 8 0 7 9
‾‾‾‾‾‾‾‾

**15.**  8 1 8 0
  2 7 5 5
+ 2 5 7 7
‾‾‾‾‾‾‾‾

**16.**  9 0 6 4
  9 6 0 7
+ 6 0 7 4
‾‾‾‾‾‾‾‾

**17.**  4 9 1 1
  2 7 5 7
+ 3 0 2 5
‾‾‾‾‾‾‾‾

**18.**  5 7 8 7
  6 9 6 2
+ 1 5 7 0
‾‾‾‾‾‾‾‾

**19.**  7 7 0 5
  5 3 2 1
+ 1 7 6 6
‾‾‾‾‾‾‾‾

**20.**  3 0 3 3
  1 4 4 7
+ 9 6 3 2
‾‾‾‾‾‾‾‾

Copyright © Mometrix Media. You have been licensed one copy of this document for personal use only. Any other reproduction or redistribution is strictly prohibited. All rights reserved.

## CHAPTER 3 - SUBTRACTION

## LESSON 1

## 2-DIGIT SUBTRACTION - BORROWING

To subtract and borrow , start with the ones column. If the bottom number is of a greater value, you have to borrow from the next column.

| Step 1: If the bottom number is a greater value than the top number, you need to borrow. | Step 2: Borrow 10 from the next column. Reducing the 8 to 7 and increasing 4 to 14. Now we are ready to subtract. | Step 3: Finish by subtracting the numbers in the tens column. |
|---|---|---|
| 84 − 19 | 7 8̸ ¹4 − 1 9 = 5 | 7 8̸ ¹4 − 1 9 = 6 5 |

### Use borrowing to solve the problems below.

1.  35
   −  6
   ‾‾‾‾
    29

2.  54
   −28

3.  83
   −  4

4.  42
   −15

5.  56
   −  9

6.  41
   −  5

7.  82
   −59

8.  16
   −  7

9.  71
   −  3

10.  52
    −28

11.  87
    −59

12.  34
    −  6

13.  72
    −35

14.  21
    −  2

15.  91
    −44

16

Copyright © Mometrix Media. You have been licensed one copy of this document for personal use only. Any other reproduction or redistribution is strictly prohibited. All rights reserved.

## LESSON 2

### SUBTRACTION WORD PROBLEMS

## Use subtraction to solve the problems below.

1.  Selena is a good soccer player. This season she has taken 38 shots at the goal and made 6 of them. How many shots has she missed this season?

2.  Billy just can't stop eating cookies. He had 62 cookies in his jar. He ate 18 of them. How many cookies are left in the jar?

3.  Aida loves baseball. She has gone to 103 games in her life. 39 were away games. How many were home games?

4.  Jonathan has collected 47 snowflakes today, but 23 of them have already melted. How many snowflakes does Jonathan have left?

Copyright © Mometrix Media. You have been licensed one copy of this document for personal use only. Any other reproduction or redistribution is strictly prohibited. All rights reserved.

## LESSON 3

## 3-DIGIT SUBTRACTION - BORROWING

To subtract and borrow, start with the ones column. If the bottom number is of a greater value, you have to borrow from the next column.

| Step 1: Any time the bottom number in a column is of greater value than the top number, you need to borrow. | Step 2: Borrow 10 from the next column. This reduces the 6 to 5 and increases the numbers in the first column from 3 to 13. | Step 3: Now we need to borrow 10 from the hundreds column. This reduces the 7 to 6 and increases the numbers in the tens column from 5 to 15. | Step 4: Finish by subtracting the numbers in all the columns. |
|---|---|---|---|
| $\begin{array}{r} 7\ 6\ 3 \\ -\ 4\ 8\ 5 \end{array}$ | $\begin{array}{r} 7\ \overset{5}{6}\ {}^{1}3 \\ -\ 4\ 8\ 5 \end{array}$ | $\begin{array}{r} \overset{6}{7}\ \overset{15}{6}\ {}^{1}3 \\ -\ 4\ 8\ 5 \end{array}$ | $\begin{array}{r} \overset{6}{7}\ \overset{15}{6}\ {}^{1}3 \\ -\ 4\ 8\ 5 \\ \hline 2\ 7\ 8 \end{array}$ |

## Use borrowing to solve the problems below.

**1.** $\begin{array}{r} 289 \\ -\ 134 \\ \hline 155 \end{array}$  **2.** $\begin{array}{r} 412 \\ -\ 389 \\ \hline \end{array}$  **3.** $\begin{array}{r} 518 \\ -\ 79 \\ \hline \end{array}$  **4.** $\begin{array}{r} 962 \\ -\ 473 \\ \hline \end{array}$  **5.** $\begin{array}{r} 412 \\ -\ 273 \\ \hline \end{array}$

**6.** $\begin{array}{r} 652 \\ -\ 386 \\ \hline \end{array}$  **7.** $\begin{array}{r} 179 \\ -\ 83 \\ \hline \end{array}$  **8.** $\begin{array}{r} 712 \\ -\ 554 \\ \hline \end{array}$  **9.** $\begin{array}{r} 369 \\ -\ 254 \\ \hline \end{array}$  **10.** $\begin{array}{r} 811 \\ -\ 632 \\ \hline \end{array}$

**11.** $\begin{array}{r} 895 \\ -\ 67 \\ \hline \end{array}$  **12.** $\begin{array}{r} 337 \\ -\ 287 \\ \hline \end{array}$  **13.** $\begin{array}{r} 615 \\ -\ 457 \\ \hline \end{array}$  **14.** $\begin{array}{r} 906 \\ -\ 687 \\ \hline \end{array}$  **15.** $\begin{array}{r} 675 \\ -\ 399 \\ \hline \end{array}$

Copyright © Mometrix Media. You have been licensed one copy of this document for personal use only. Any other reproduction or redistribution is strictly prohibited. All rights reserved.

## LESSON 4

## 4-DIGIT SUBTRACTION - BORROWING

Use what you learned about borrowing to
solve the problems below.

1.  6,432
  − 5,320
  ‾‾‾‾‾‾‾
    1,112

2.  2,675
  − 1,564
  ‾‾‾‾‾‾‾

3.  4,233
  −   452
  ‾‾‾‾‾‾‾

4.  5,428
  − 2,649
  ‾‾‾‾‾‾‾

5.  1,995
  −   239
  ‾‾‾‾‾‾‾

6.  7,321
  −   834
  ‾‾‾‾‾‾‾

7.  9,211
  − 1,700
  ‾‾‾‾‾‾‾

8.  3,946
  − 1,682
  ‾‾‾‾‾‾‾

9.  2,463
  − 1,939
  ‾‾‾‾‾‾‾

10.  8,959
   − 3,274
   ‾‾‾‾‾‾‾

11.  1,295
   −   968
   ‾‾‾‾‾‾‾

12.  9,942
   − 7,895
   ‾‾‾‾‾‾‾

13.  7,542
   − 2,907
   ‾‾‾‾‾‾‾

14.  3,649
   − 1,590
   ‾‾‾‾‾‾‾

15.  9,864
   − 4,389
   ‾‾‾‾‾‾‾

16.  3,888
   −   999
   ‾‾‾‾‾‾‾

17.  5,001
   − 3,547
   ‾‾‾‾‾‾‾

18.  1,775
   −   859
   ‾‾‾‾‾‾‾

19.  3,880
   − 1,125
   ‾‾‾‾‾‾‾

20.  9,567
   − 6,820
   ‾‾‾‾‾‾‾

Copyright © Mometrix Media. You have been licensed one copy of this document for personal use only. Any other reproduction or redistribution is strictly prohibited. All rights reserved.

## CHAPTER 4 - DECIMALS

## LESSON 1

## ADDING DECIMALS

Adding decimals is like most normal addition. You just have to remember to line up the decimals.

**Hint:** Decimal points always go at the end of a whole number (3 = 3.0 or 3.00)

| **Example:** Add 2.43, 4.5 and 3 | | |
|---|---|---|
| **Step 1:**<br>Line up the numbers | **Step 2:**<br>Add zeros | **Step 3:**<br>Find the total |
| 2.43<br>4.5<br>+ 3 | 2.43<br>4.50<br>+ 3.00 | 2.43<br>4.50<br>+ 3.00<br>9.93 |

### Line up the numbers and solve the problems below.
### Show your work in the boxes.

**1:** 1.21 + 2.33 + .05

$$\begin{array}{r} 1.21 \\ 2.33 \\ + \phantom{0}.05 \\ \hline 3.59 \end{array}$$

**2:** 4 + 1.63 + 2.20

**3:** .24 + 4.87 + 11

**4:** 7.12 + 2.04 + 5

**5:** 9.11 + .43 + .89

**6:** 64 + 8.79 + 1.57

Copyright © Mometrix Media. You have been licensed one copy of this document for personal use only. Any other reproduction or redistribution is strictly prohibited. All rights reserved.

## LESSON 2

### ADDING DECIMALS WORD PROBLEMS

**Solve the problems below.**

1. Jimmie's water gun can hold 30.08 ounces of water. Steven's water gun can hold 22.56 ounces. How many ounces of water do they have together?

_____

2. Sara walks every afternoon. On Monday she walked 2.3 miles. On Tuesday she walked 1.8 miles. On Wednesday she walked 3.1 miles. How many miles did she walk in total?

_____

3. Mickey loves to race his bike. In race one he had a finishing time of 13.38 minutes. In race two he had a finishing time of 12.58 minutes. In race three he had a finishing time of 12.32 minutes. What was his total time for all the races?

_____

4. Mary can carry 6.75 pounds of dirt in her wagon. Mark can carry 8.25 pounds in his wagon. How much dirt can they carry in total?

_____

Copyright © Mometrix Media. You have been licensed one copy of this document for personal use only. Any other reproduction or redistribution is strictly prohibited. All rights reserved.

## LESSON 3

## ROUNDING DECIMALS

To round numbers with decimal points look at the numbers to right of the decimal. If it has a value of higher than 5 round the number to the left of the decimal up.

$$6.8 = 7$$

If the number to the right of the decimal is less than 5, round the number down.

$$6.3 = 6$$

### Round each decimal to the nearest whole number.

1. 9 2.8 = __93__

2. 1 2.5 = _____

3. 3 3.1 = _____

4. 2 4.9 = _____

5. 5 7.7 = _____

6. 6 5.1 = _____

7. 8 2.5 = _____

8. 4 1.6 = _____

9. 6 8.6 = _____

10. 2 0.4 = _____

11. 3 4.2 = _____

12. 3 1.8 = _____

13. 7 6.7 = _____

13. 7 2.2 = _____

15. 1 2.3 = _____

16. 4 3.7 = _____

17. 4 5.8 = _____

18. 5 5.9 = _____

19. 2 1.4 = _____

20. 1 9.3 = _____

Copyright © Mometrix Media. You have been licensed one copy of this document for personal use only. Any other reproduction or redistribution is strictly prohibited. All rights reserved.

## LESSON 4

## SUBTRACTING DECIMALS

Subtracting decimals is like normal subtraction.
You just have to remember to line up the decimals.

**Hint:** Decimal points always go at the end of a whole number ( 6 = 6.0 or 6.00 )

| **Example:** Subtract 5.7 from 9.39 | | |
|---|---|---|
| **Step 1:**<br>Line up the decimals. | **Step 2:**<br>Add zeros and borrow<br>when needed. | **Step 3:**<br>Subtract all the<br>numbers. |
| 9.39<br>− 5.7 | $\overset{8}{\cancel{9}}.^{1}39$<br>− 5.70 | $\overset{8}{\cancel{9}}.^{1}39$<br>− 5.70<br>3.69 |

### Line up the numbers and solve the problems below.
### Show your work in the boxes.

1. 6.05 - 3.89

```
  6.05
- 3.89
──────
  2.16
```

2. 48.27 - 13.65

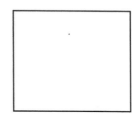

3. 8.55 - 3.9

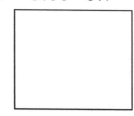

4. 331 - 4.72

5. 902.22 - 47.79

6. 75.5 - 6.51

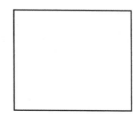

Copyright © Mometrix Media. You have been licensed one copy of this document for personal use only. Any other reproduction or redistribution is strictly prohibited. All rights reserved.

## LESSON 5

### SUBTRACTING DECIMALS WORD PROBLEMS

**Use subtraction to solve the problems below.**

1. Pete wants a new teddy bear. His mom is going to help him buy one. A new bear costs $19.50. Pete has $7.32. How much money does he need to get from mom?

_____

2. Tammy wants a new jump rope. She has $3.78. The jump rope costs $6.99. How much more money does she need?

_____

3. Randy and John want a new toy truck. The toy truck costs $13.75. Randy has $4.15 and John has $6.42. How much more money do they need?

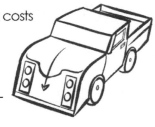

_____

4. Eric sold his old pogo stick for $5.89. A new one costs $35.99. How much more money does Eric need?

_____

Copyright © Mometrix Media. You have been licensed one copy of this document for personal use only. Any other reproduction or redistribution is strictly prohibited. All rights reserved.

## CHAPTER 5 - MULTIPLICATION

## LESSON 1

## MULTIPLICATION TABLES 1

| X | 1 | 2 | 3 |
|---|---|---|---|
| 1 | 1 | 2 | 3 |
| 2 | 2 | 4 | 6 |

This is a multiplication table. Multiply the numbers in the top row by the numbers in the side row.

**1.**

| X | 1 | 2 | 3 | 4 | 5 |
|---|---|---|---|---|---|
| 6 | | | | | |
| 7 | | | | | |
| 8 | | | | | |

**2.**

| X | 7 | 8 | 9 |
|---|---|---|---|
| 4 | | | |
| 5 | | | |
| 6 | | | |
| 7 | | | |
| 8 | | | |

**3.**

| X | 9 | 10 | 11 |
|---|---|----|----|
| 7 | | | |
| 8 | | | |
| 9 | | | |
| 10 | | | |
| 11 | | | |

**4.**

| X | 2 | 3 | 4 | 5 | 6 |
|---|---|---|---|---|---|
| 20 | | | | | |
| 25 | | | | | |
| 27 | | | | | |

25

Copyright © Mometrix Media. You have been licensed one copy of this document for personal use only. Any other reproduction or redistribution is strictly prohibited. All rights reserved.

## LESSON 2

## MULTIPLYING 1-DIGIT NUMBERS BY 2-DIGIT NUMBERS

To multiply a one-digit number by a two-digit number, start in the ones place and then use basic multiplication rules.

| | Tens | Ones |
|---|---|---|
| **Step 1:** Multiply the numbers in the ones place | 4 | 3 |
| | x | 2 |
| | | 6 |

| | Tens | Ones |
|---|---|---|
| **Step 2:** Multiply the numbers in the tens place | 4 | 3 |
| | x | 2 |
| | 8 | 6 |

### Solve the problems below.

1. 2 4
   x 2
   ───
   4 8

2. 3 1
   x 3
   ───

3. 4 3
   x 2
   ───

4. 1 1
   x 7
   ───

5. 1 1
   x 5
   ───

6. 4 4
   x 2
   ───

7. 1 1
   x 9
   ───

8. 1 8
   x 1
   ───

9. 2 1
   x 4
   ───

10. 2 2
    x 3
    ───

Copyright © Mometrix Media. You have been licensed one copy of this document for personal use only. Any other reproduction or redistribution is strictly prohibited. All rights reserved.

## LESSON 3

## MULTIPLYING BY 10s

Multiplying by ten is just like regular two-digit number multiplication, but there is just one extra step. You bring the zero down first; this adds it to the end of the number.

| Hundreds | Tens | Ones |
|---|---|---|
| | 5 | 4 |
| x | 1 | 0 |
| | | [0] |

| Hundreds | Tens | Ones |
|---|---|---|
| | 5 | 4 |
| x | 1 | 0 |
| | [4] | 0 |

| Hundreds | Tens | Ones |
|---|---|---|
| | 5 | 4 |
| x | 1 | 0 |
| [5] | 4 | 0 |

### Solve the problems below.

1.  2 6
    x 1 0
    ———
    2 6 0

2.  7 1
    x 1 0
    ———

3.  6 7
    x 1 0
    ———

4.  2 2
    x 1 0
    ———

5.  3 8
    x 1 0
    ———

6.  8 4
    x 1 0
    ———

7.  1 9
    x 1 0
    ———

8.  1 8
    x 1 0
    ———

9.  9 4
    x 1 0
    ———

10. 2 9
    x 1 0
    ———

Copyright © Mometrix Media. You have been licensed one copy of this document for personal use only. Any other reproduction or redistribution is strictly prohibited. All rights reserved.

## LESSON 4

## MULTIPLYING 1-DIGIT NUMBERS BY 2-DIGIT NUMBERS - REGROUPING

To multiply a one-digit number by a two-digit number with regrouping, start in the ones place and then use basic multiplication rules. When the number equals ten or more, the first digit carries over to the next spot. This is called **regrouping**.

| | Hundreds | Tens | Ones |
|---|---|---|---|
| **Step 1:** Multiply the numbers in the ones column and carry the first digit over to the tens column. | | 2 4 | 7 3 |
| x | | | |

$3 \times 7 = 21$

| | Hundreds | Tens | Ones |
|---|---|---|---|
| **Step 2:** Multiply the digit in at the bottom of the ones column by the digit in the tens column and add the regrouped number. | | 2 + 4 | 7 3 |
| x | | 4 | 1 |

$4 \times 3 = 12$   Then $12 + 2 = 14$

| | Hundreds | Tens | Ones |
|---|---|---|---|
| **Step 3:** The one then carries over to the hundreds place. | | 2 4 | 7 3 |
| x | 1 | 4 | 1 |

Answer = 141

### Solve the problems below.

1.  46
    x  2
    ────
    9 2

2.  58
    x  7

3.  43
    x  4

4.  87
    x  3

5.  36
    x  5

6.  44
    x  5

7.  32
    x  9

8.  55
    x  9

9.  99
    x  2

10.  59
     x  6

Copyright © Mometrix Media. You have been licensed one copy of this document for personal use only. Any other reproduction or redistribution is strictly prohibited. All rights reserved.

## LESSON 5

## MULTIPLYING 1-DIGIT NUMBERS BY 3-DIGIT NUMBERS - REGROUPING

To multiply a one-digit number by a three-digit number, start in the ones place and then use basic multiplication rules.

| | Hundreds | Tens | Ones |
|---|---|---|---|
| **Step 1:** First multiply the top digit in the ones column by the bottom digit in the ones column. | 2 | 3 | 3 |
| x | | | 3 |
| | | | 9 |

3 x 3 = 9

| | Hundreds | Tens | Ones |
|---|---|---|---|
| **Step 2:** Next multiply the digit in the tens column by the bottom digit in the ones column. | 2 | 3 | 3 |
| x | | | 3 |
| | | 9 | 9 |

3 x 3 = 9

| | Hundreds | Tens | Ones |
|---|---|---|---|
| **Step 3:** Next multiply the digit in the hundreds column by the bottom digit in the ones column. | 2 | 3 | 3 |
| x | | | 3 |
| | 6 | 9 | 9 |

2 x 3 = 6

**Answer** = 699

### Solve the problems below.

**1.**  1 4 2
   x   2
  ———
   2 8 4

**2.**  2 2 1
   x   3
  ———

**3.**  3 4 1
   x   2
  ———

**4.**  1 2 1
   x   4
  ———

**5.**  6 9 8
   x   1
  ———

**6.**  2 1 2
   x   4
  ———

**7.**  1 3 2
   x   3
  ———

**8.**  2 3 3
   x   2
  ———

**9.**  2 3 2
   x   3
  ———

**10.**  1 4 1
   x   2
  ———

**11.**  2 1 2
   x   3
  ———

**12.**  1 1 2
   x   3
  ———

29

Copyright © Mometrix Media. You have been licensed one copy of this document for personal use only. Any other reproduction or redistribution is strictly prohibited. All rights reserved.

## LESSON 6

## MULTIPLYING 2-DIGIT NUMBERS BY 2-DIGIT NUMBERS - REGROUPING

To multiply a two-digit number by a two-digit number, start in the ones place and then use basic multiplication and addition rules. Dont forget to use what you learned about regrouping.

| 1. Multiply by the **ones** multiplier. | 2. Multiply by the **tens** multiplier. | 3. Add the products. |
|---|---|---|
| $$\begin{array}{r} \overset{2}{4}\,6 \\ \times\ 2\,4 \\ \hline 1\,0\,4 \end{array}$$ | $$\begin{array}{r} \overset{1}{4}\,6 \\ \times\ 2\,4 \\ \hline 1\,8\,4 \\ +\,9\,2\,0 \end{array}$$ | $$\begin{array}{r} 4\,6 \\ \times\ 2\,4 \\ \hline 1\,8\,4 \\ +\,9\,2\,0 \\ \hline 1\,1\,0\,4 \end{array}$$ |
| **4 is the first multiplier** <br> 4 x 46 = 104 | **20 is the second multiplier** <br> 20 x 46 = 104 | **Add the two products** <br> 184 + 920 = 1104 |

### Solve the problems below.

**1.**
$$\begin{array}{r} 49 \\ \times\ 15 \\ \hline 245 \\ +\,490 \\ \hline 735 \end{array}$$

**2.**
$$\begin{array}{r} 13 \\ \times\ 12 \\ \hline \end{array}$$

**3.**
$$\begin{array}{r} 54 \\ \times\ 22 \\ \hline \end{array}$$

**4.**
$$\begin{array}{r} 72 \\ \times\ 45 \\ \hline \end{array}$$

**5.**
$$\begin{array}{r} 38 \\ \times\ 25 \\ \hline \end{array}$$

**6.**
$$\begin{array}{r} 84 \\ \times\ 55 \\ \hline \end{array}$$

**7.**
$$\begin{array}{r} 69 \\ \times\ 37 \\ \hline \end{array}$$

**8.**
$$\begin{array}{r} 29 \\ \times\ 23 \\ \hline \end{array}$$

**9.**
$$\begin{array}{r} 79 \\ \times\ 56 \\ \hline \end{array}$$

**10.**
$$\begin{array}{r} 99 \\ \times\ 56 \\ \hline \end{array}$$

Copyright © Mometrix Media. You have been licensed one copy of this document for personal use only. Any other reproduction or redistribution is strictly prohibited. All rights reserved.

## CHAPTER 6 - DIVISION

## LESSON 1

## DIVISION

- Division is a way to find out how many times one number is counted in another number.

- The $\div$ sign means "divided by".

- Another way to divide is to use $\overline{)}$ .

- The dividend is the larger number that is divided by the smaller number, the divisor.

- The answer of a division problem is called the quotient.

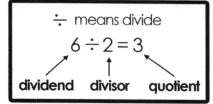

$\div$ means divide

$$6 \div 2 = 3$$

**dividend    divisor    quotient**

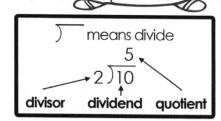

$\overline{)}$ means divide

$$2\overline{)10}^{\,5}$$

**divisor    dividend    quotient**

- $6 \div 2 = 3$ is read "6 divided by 2 is equal to 3".

- In $6 \div 2 = 3$, the divisor is 2, the dividend is 6 and the quotient is 3.

- $2\overline{)10}^{\,5}$ is read "10 divided by 2 is equal to 5".

- In $2\overline{)10}^{\,5}$ , the divisor is 2, the dividend is 10 and the quotient is 5.

Copyright © Mometrix Media. You have been licensed one copy of this document for personal use only. Any other reproduction or redistribution is strictly prohibited. All rights reserved.

**LESSON 2**

**BASIC DIVISION**

Divide these problems.

1.  $7\overline{)21}$ with $3$ above

2.  $6\overline{)48}$

3.  $2\overline{)12}$

4.  $7\overline{)28}$

5.  $4\overline{)36}$

6.  $3\overline{)21}$

7.  $7\overline{)21}$

8.  $5\overline{)40}$

9.  $5\overline{)15}$

10. $2\overline{)6}$

11. $8\overline{)72}$

12. $10\overline{)100}$

13. $8\overline{)32}$

14. $5\overline{)25}$

15. $5\overline{)5}$

16. $8\overline{)88}$

17. $8\overline{)56}$

18. $5\overline{)75}$

19. $3\overline{)9}$

20. $4\overline{)32}$

Copyright © Mometrix Media. You have been licensed one copy of this document for personal use only. Any other reproduction or redistribution is strictly prohibited. All rights reserved.

## LESSON 3

## DIVISION WITH REMAINDERS

- Sometimes groups of objects or numbers cannot be divided into equal groups.
- The number left over in a division problem is called the remainder.
- The remainder must be smaller than the divisor.

If we divide 13 🍎 into groups of 5, you get 2 equal groups

and 3 🍎 left over. These are the **remainders**.

This is how you write it out. →

$$5\overline{)13} \quad \begin{array}{r} 2\,r\,3 \\ -10 \\ \hline 3 \end{array}$$

Remainders

---

### Divide these problems. Some may not have remainders.

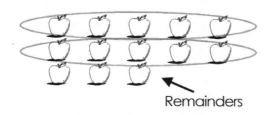

1. $\begin{array}{r} 2\,r\,2 \\ 3\overline{)8} \\ -6 \\ \hline 2 \end{array}$

2. $7\overline{)35}$

3. $6\overline{)25}$

4. $8\overline{)39}$

5. $5\overline{)52}$

6. $9\overline{)85}$

7. $5\overline{)61}$

8. $3\overline{)43}$

Copyright © Mometrix Media. You have been licensed one copy of this document for personal use only. Any other reproduction or redistribution is strictly prohibited. All rights reserved.

**LESSON 4**

**DIVISION - FILL IN THE BLANKS**

Use division to fill in the boxes on the problems below.

1.  $4\overline{)36}$    9

2.  $6\overline{)\phantom{0}}$    9

3.  $4\overline{)\phantom{0}}$    15

4.  $5\overline{)\phantom{0}}$    20

5.  $3\overline{)\phantom{0}}$    2

6.  $7\overline{)\phantom{0}}$    7

7.  $2\overline{)\phantom{0}}$    5

8.  $9\overline{)\phantom{0}}$    5

9.  $8\overline{)\phantom{0}}$    8

10. $9\overline{)\phantom{0}}$    32

11. $7\overline{)\phantom{0}}$    9

12. $3\overline{)\phantom{0}}$    11

13. $6\overline{)\phantom{0}}$    9

14. $4\overline{)\phantom{0}}$    6

34

Copyright © Mometrix Media. You have been licensed one copy of this document for personal use only. Any other reproduction or redistribution is strictly prohibited. All rights reserved.

## LESSON 5

## DIVISION WORD PROBLEMS

### Use division to solve the problems below.

1. Rachel bought three pairs of ballet shoes for $99. What is the cost of each pair of shoes?

_____

2. Charlie has 21 kids in his class. If he divides the kids into 3 groups how many kids will be in each group?

_____

3. Sara loves her dolls; she has 12 of them. If she divides them into groups of 4, how many dolls will be in each group?

_____

4. Harry has 72 toy trucks and cars. If he divides them into groups of 8, how many cars and trucks will be in each group?

_____

Copyright © Mometrix Media. You have been licensed one copy of this document for personal use only. Any other reproduction or redistribution is strictly prohibited. All rights reserved.

## LESSON 6

## 2-DIGIT QUOTIENTS

| Estimate | Divide the tens | Bring down the ones and repeat the steps. | The answer is: **23 r 3** |
|---|---|---|---|
| $\dfrac{2}{4)\overline{95}}$ | $\begin{array}{r} 2 \\ 4)\overline{95} \\ -8 \\ \hline 1 \end{array}$ | $\begin{array}{r} 23 \\ 4)\overline{95} \\ -8\downarrow \\ \hline 15 \\ -12 \\ \hline 3 \end{array}$ | Remember these steps: |
| Take a look at the first digit. Estimate how many times 4 will go into 9 without going over the number. | 4 can go into 9 twice. Multiply 4 x 2 and get 8. Subtract the 8 from 9 leaving 1. | Bring down the 5 from the one's column and repeat the steps. **The remainder is 3** | 1. Divide<br>2. Multiply<br>3. Subtract<br>4. Bring down<br><br>Repeat these steps until there are no more digits to bring down. |

### Divide these problems. Some may not have remainders.

1.
$$\begin{array}{r} 28\,r1 \\ 2)\overline{57} \\ -4 \\ \hline 17 \\ -16 \\ \hline 1 \end{array}$$

2.  $3)\overline{72}$

3.  $4)\overline{65}$

4.  $3)\overline{86}$

5.  $2)\overline{37}$

6.  $7)\overline{93}$

7.  $5)\overline{73}$

8.  $7)\overline{98}$

Copyright © Mometrix Media. You have been licensed one copy of this document for personal use only. Any other reproduction or redistribution is strictly prohibited. All rights reserved.

## Lesson 7

## Dividing 3-Digit Numbers

When dividing a three-digit number by a two-digit number, the quotient may have two or three digits. Here are some examples:

| Estimate | Divide | Estimate | Divide |
|---|---|---|---|
| $\begin{array}{r} 200 \\ 3\overline{)719} \end{array}$ | $\begin{array}{r} 239\,r2 \\ 3\overline{)719} \\ \underline{-6} \\ 11 \\ \underline{-9} \\ 29 \\ \underline{-27} \\ 2 \end{array}$ | $\begin{array}{r} 70 \\ 3\overline{)235} \end{array}$ | $\begin{array}{r} 78\,r1 \\ 3\overline{)235} \\ \underline{-21} \\ 25 \\ \underline{-24} \\ 1 \end{array}$ |

1. Divide
2. Multiply
3. Subtract
4. Compare
5. Bring down

**Repeat the steps as needed**

1. Divide
2. Multiply
3. Subtract
4. Compare
5. Bring down

**Repeat the steps as needed**

### Divide these problems. Some may not have remainders.

1. $\begin{array}{r} 246\,r\,3 \\ 4\overline{)987} \\ \underline{-8} \\ 18 \\ \underline{-16} \\ 27 \\ \underline{-24} \\ 3 \end{array}$

2. $6\overline{)297}$

3. $2\overline{)592}$

4. $3\overline{)769}$

5. $4\overline{)867}$

6. $5\overline{)934}$

Copyright © Mometrix Media. You have been licensed one copy of this document for personal use only. Any other reproduction or redistribution is strictly prohibited. All rights reserved.

## LESSON 8

### AVERAGING

An average is found by adding two or more quantities together
and dividing by the number of quantities.

**Step 1**: Find the sum of the quantities ⟶ $35 + 15 + 10 = 60$

**Step 2**: Divide by the number of
quantities ⟶ $60 \div 3 = \boxed{20}$

**Work the problems out. Find the average of each set of numbers.**

1. $6, 12, 15 = \underline{\ 11\ }$
$$
\begin{array}{r}
6 \\
12 \\
+\ 15 \\
\hline
33 \div 3 = \boxed{11}
\end{array}
$$

2. $1, 13, 9, 65 = \underline{\qquad}$

3. $2, 7, 11, 12 = \underline{\qquad}$

4. $48, 23, 28 = \underline{\qquad}$

5. $2, 29, 35, 18 = \underline{\qquad}$

6. $9, 33, 17, 29 = \underline{\qquad}$

Copyright © Mometrix Media. You have been licensed one copy of this document for personal use only. Any other reproduction or redistribution is strictly prohibited. All rights reserved.

## LESSON 9

### AVERAGING WORD PROBLEMS

**Write out each averaging problem and solve.**

1. Jamie wants to know her average test score in math class. On her 4 tests she scored 79, 86, 92 and 80. What is her average test score?

2. Steven scored 17, 16, 19, 27, 21 points in 5 games. How many points did he average?

3. Kenny is good at video games. He played the game 6 times. He scored 128, 58, 166, 164, 212 and 72. What is his average score?

Copyright © Mometrix Media. You have been licensed one copy of this document for personal use only. Any other reproduction or redistribution is strictly prohibited. All rights reserved.

## CHAPTER 7 - GEOMETRY

## LESSON 1

## FLAT SHAPES

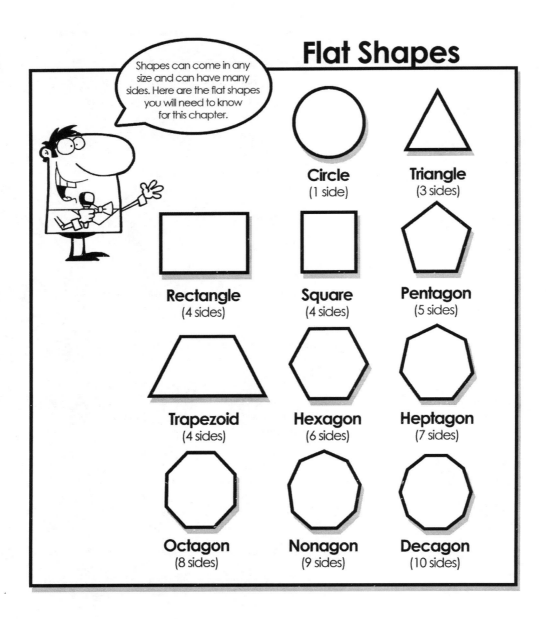

Copyright © Mometrix Media. You have been licensed one copy of this document for personal use only. Any other reproduction or redistribution is strictly prohibited. All rights reserved.

**IDENTIFYING FLAT SHAPES**

Write the number of sides in each box below.
Write the name of each shape in the blanks.

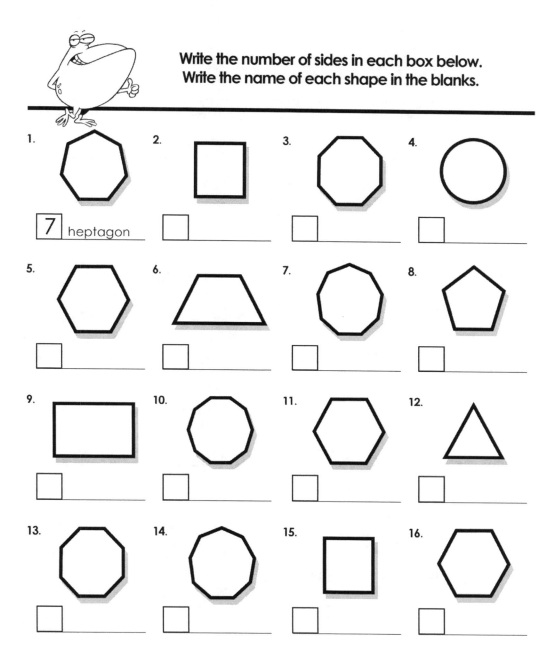

1. [ 7 ] heptagon

2.

3.

4.

5.

6.

7.

8.

9.

10.

11.

12.

13.

14.

15.

16.

41

Copyright © Mometrix Media. You have been licensed one copy of this document for personal use only. Any other reproduction or redistribution is strictly prohibited. All rights reserved.

**LESSON 2**

**SOLID SHAPE**

# Solid Shapes

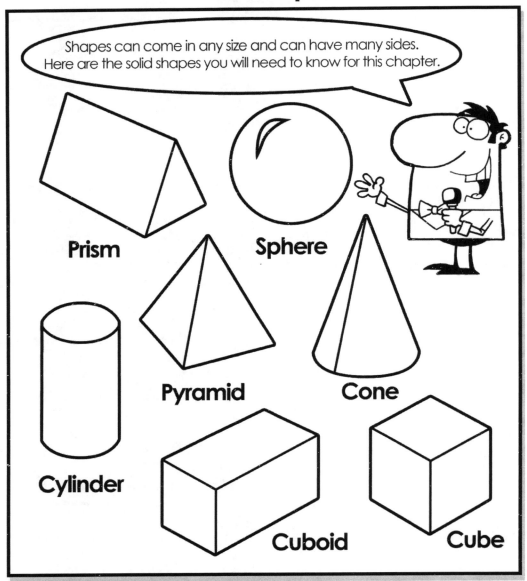

Copyright © Mometrix Media. You have been licensed one copy of this document for personal use only. Any other reproduction or redistribution is strictly prohibited. All rights reserved.

## IDENTIFYING SOLID SHAPE

Identify each shape below and write the names in the blanks.

1.

cube
_____

2.

_____

3.

_____

4.

_____

5.

_____

6.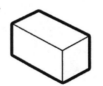

_____

7.

_____

8.

_____

9.

_____

10.

_____

11.

_____

12.

_____

13.

_____

14.

_____

15.

_____

16.

_____

Copyright © Mometrix Media. You have been licensed one copy of this document for personal use only. Any other reproduction or redistribution is strictly prohibited. All rights reserved.

## LESSON 3

### IDENTIFYING TRIANGLES

Triangles can come in many shapes. Here are some examples.

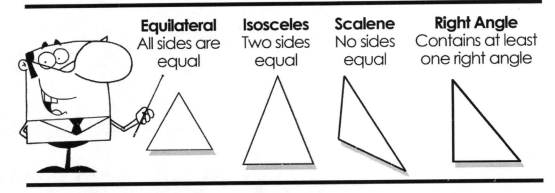

**Equilateral**
All sides are equal

**Isosceles**
Two sides equal

**Scalene**
No sides equal

**Right Angle**
Contains at least one right angle

Name each triangle as an **equilateral**, **isosceles**, **scalene** or **right** triangle.

1.

isosceles

2.
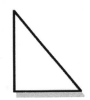
_____

3.

_____

4.

_____

5.

_____

6.

_____

7.

_____

8.

_____

Copyright © Mometrix Media. You have been licensed one copy of this document for personal use only. Any other reproduction or redistribution is strictly prohibited. All rights reserved.

## LESSON 4

## IDENTIFYING POINTS, LINES AND RAYS

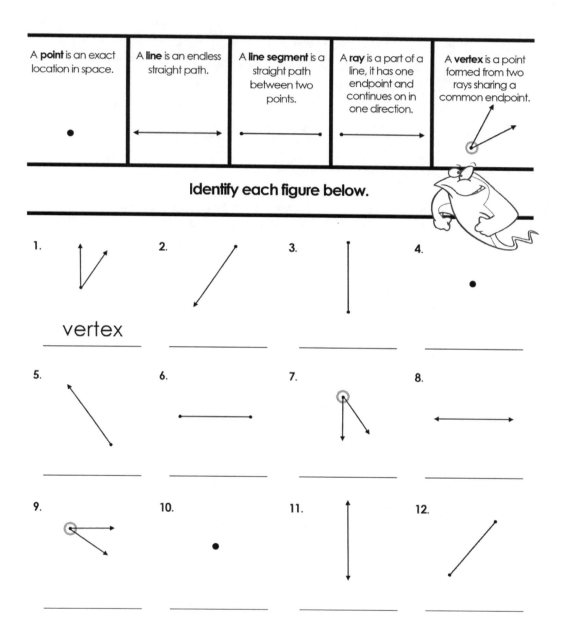

| A **point** is an exact location in space. | A **line** is an endless straight path. | A **line segment** is a straight path between two points. | A **ray** is a part of a line, it has one endpoint and continues on in one direction. | A **vertex** is a point formed from two rays sharing a common endpoint. |
|---|---|---|---|---|

### Identify each figure below.

1.

vertex

2.

3.

4.

5.

6.

7.

8.

9.

10.

11.

12.

45

Copyright © Mometrix Media. You have been licensed one copy of this document for personal use only. Any other reproduction or redistribution is strictly prohibited. All rights reserved.

## LESSON 5

### IDENTIFYING PARALLEL AND PERPENDICULAR LINES

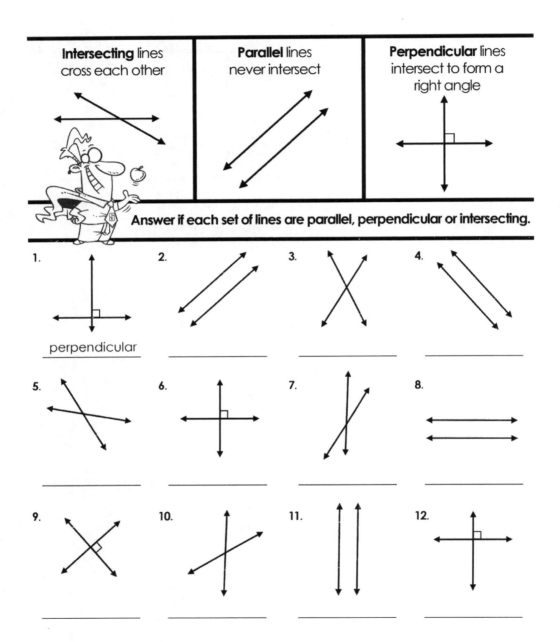

| Intersecting lines cross each other | Parallel lines never intersect | Perpendicular lines intersect to form a right angle |
|---|---|---|

**Answer if each set of lines are parallel, perpendicular or intersecting.**

1. perpendicular

2. _____

3. _____

4. _____

5. _____

6. _____

7. _____

8. _____

9. _____

10. _____

11. _____

12. _____

Copyright © Mometrix Media. You have been licensed one copy of this document for personal use only. Any other reproduction or redistribution is strictly prohibited. All rights reserved.

## LESSON 6

## IDENTIFYING ANGLES

Angles are where two lines meet.

| | | |
|---|---|---|
| 90° | 45° | 110° |
| An angle that is exactly 90° is a **right angle**. | An angle that is less than 90° is an **acute angle**. | An angle that is more than 90° is an **obtuse angle**. |

Identify if each angle is a **right**, **acute** or **obtuse** angle.

1.

obtuse
_____

2.

_____

3.

_____

4.

_____

5.

_____

6.

_____

7.

_____

8.

_____

9.

_____

10.

_____

11.

_____

12.

_____

47

Copyright © Mometrix Media. You have been licensed one copy of this document for personal use only. Any other reproduction or redistribution is strictly prohibited. All rights reserved.

**LESSON 7**

**FINDING AREA**

Area is the measurement of a shape's surface area.
To find the **area** of a shape, multiply the length by the width.

**24 ft.**

**8 ft.**

Area = 24 ft. x 8 ft. = 192 ft.
Area = 192 sq. ft.

## Find the area of each shape. Write the problem out.

**1.**

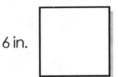

6 in.

6 in.

6 x 6 = 36 sq. in.

**2.**

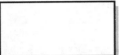

3 ft.

12 ft.

**3.**

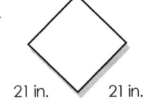

21 in.        21 in.

**4.**

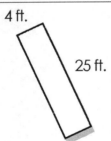

4 ft.

25 ft.

**5.**

12 yd.        12 yd.

**6.**

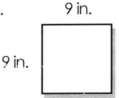

9 in.

9 in.

Copyright © Mometrix Media. You have been licensed one copy of this document for personal use only. Any other reproduction or redistribution is strictly prohibited. All rights reserved.

## LESSON 8

## FINDING PERIMETER

**Perimeter** is the distance around an object.
Find the perimeter of each object by adding all the sides.

**12** in.

**10** in. ☐ **10** in.     **Perimeter** = 12 in. + 12 in. + 10 in. + 10 in.

**12** in.          **Perimeter** = 44 in.

### Find the perimeter of each shape. Write the problem out.

20 yd.

**1.**  ☐  50 yd. ☐ 50 yd.

20 yd.

20 + 50 + 20 + 50 = 140yd.

2 ft.

**2.** 10 ft. ☐ 8 ft.

5 ft.

**3.** 100 in. ◁ 88 in.

57 in.

20 ft.

**4.** 45 ft. ☐ 45 ft.

15 ft.

34 in.

**5.** 37 in. ☐ 75 in.

29 in.

**6.** 68 yd. △ 68 yd.

27 yd.

Copyright © Mometrix Media. You have been licensed one copy of this document for personal use only. Any other reproduction or redistribution is strictly prohibited. All rights reserved.

## LESSON 9

### UNDERSTANDING VOLUME

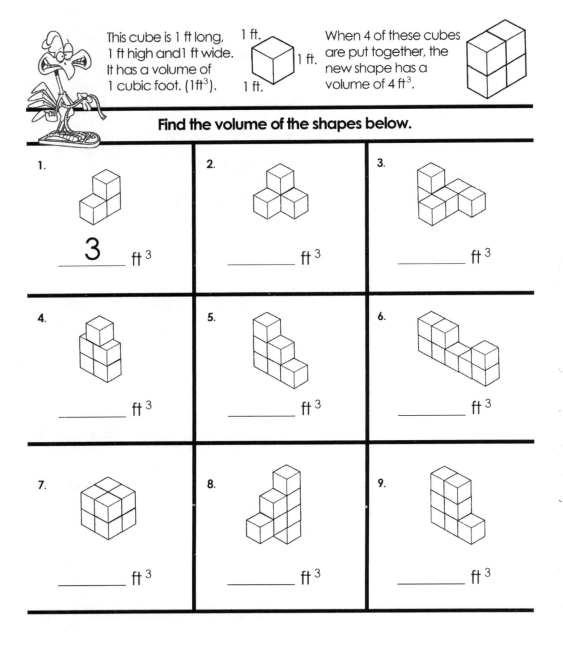

This cube is 1 ft long, 1 ft high and 1 ft wide. It has a volume of 1 cubic foot. (1ft³).

1 ft.
1 ft.
1 ft.

When 4 of these cubes are put together, the new shape has a volume of 4 ft³.

### Find the volume of the shapes below.

1.

___3___ ft³

2.

_____ ft³

3.

_____ ft³

4.

_____ ft³

5.

_____ ft³

6.

_____ ft³

7.

_____ ft³

8.

_____ ft³

9.

_____ ft³

Copyright © Mometrix Media. You have been licensed one copy of this document for personal use only. Any other reproduction or redistribution is strictly prohibited. All rights reserved.

## CHAPTER 8 - MEASUREMENTS

## LESSON 1

## MEASUREMENT

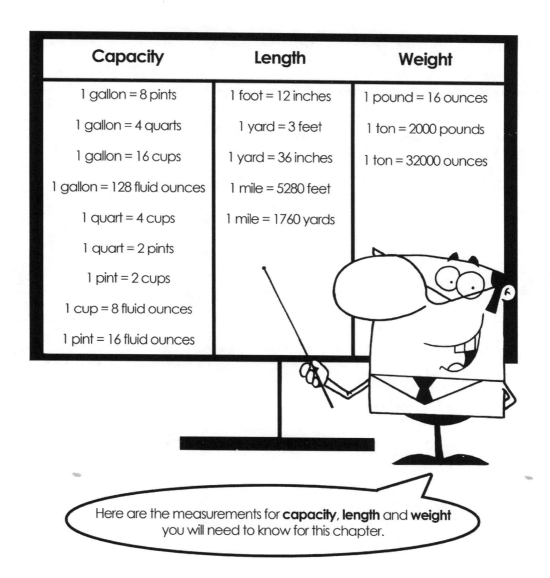

| Capacity | Length | Weight |
|---|---|---|
| 1 gallon = 8 pints | 1 foot = 12 inches | 1 pound = 16 ounces |
| 1 gallon = 4 quarts | 1 yard = 3 feet | 1 ton = 2000 pounds |
| 1 gallon = 16 cups | 1 yard = 36 inches | 1 ton = 32000 ounces |
| 1 gallon = 128 fluid ounces | 1 mile = 5280 feet | |
| 1 quart = 4 cups | 1 mile = 1760 yards | |
| 1 quart = 2 pints | | |
| 1 pint = 2 cups | | |
| 1 cup = 8 fluid ounces | | |
| 1 pint = 16 fluid ounces | | |

Here are the measurements for **capacity**, **length** and **weight** you will need to know for this chapter.

Copyright © Mometrix Media. You have been licensed one copy of this document for personal use only. Any other reproduction or redistribution is strictly prohibited. All rights reserved.

## LESSON 2

### OUNCES, POUNDS AND TONS

One - half pound (lb.) = 8 ounces (oz.)
1 pound (lb.) = 16 ounces (oz.)
One - half ton (T.) = 1,000 pounds (lb.)
1 ton (T.) = 2,000 pounds (lb.)

**Complete the problems below.**

 **1.** 48 oz. = ___3___ lb.

 **2.** 32 lb. = _____ oz.

 **3.** 4,000 lb. = _____ T.

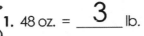 **4.** 80 oz. = _____ lb.

 **5.** 2 lb. = _____ oz.

 **6.** 8 lb. = _____ oz.

 **7.** 3T. = _____ lb.

 **8.** 6 lb. = _____ oz.

 **9.** 16 oz. = _____ lb.

 **10.** 12,000 lb. = _____ T.

52

Copyright © Mometrix Media. You have been licensed one copy of this document for personal use only. Any other reproduction or redistribution is strictly prohibited. All rights reserved.

## LESSON 3

### INCHES, FEET AND YARDS

| 12 inches = 1 foot | 3 feet = 1 yard |
|---|---|
| 36 inches = 1 yard | |

---

### Compare inches to feet.

Use the symbols **<**, **>**, and **=** to answer the questions below

1.  10 feet **>** 100 inches       2.  20 inches ____ 3 feet

3.  12 inches ____ 1 foot          4.  6 feet ____ 50 inches

5.  40 inches ____ 3 feet          6.  5 feet ____ 70 inches

7.  4 feet ____ 48 inches          8.  72 inches ____ 6 feet

---

### Compare inches, feet, and yards.

Use the symbols **<**, **>**, and **=** to answer the questions below

9.  9 feet ____ 32 yards          10.  46 inches ____ 2 yards

11.  40 feet ____ 3 yards         12.  4 yards ____ 15 feet

13.  4 feet ____ 100 inches       14.  1 foot ____ 2 yards

15.  24 inches ____ 1 foot        16.  6 yards ____ 24 feet

Copyright © Mometrix Media. You have been licensed one copy of this document for personal use only. Any other reproduction or redistribution is strictly prohibited. All rights reserved.

## LESSON 4

### RULER MEASUREMENT - INCHES

Measure each object to the nearest $\frac{1}{2}$ or $\frac{1}{4}$ inch using the rulers below.

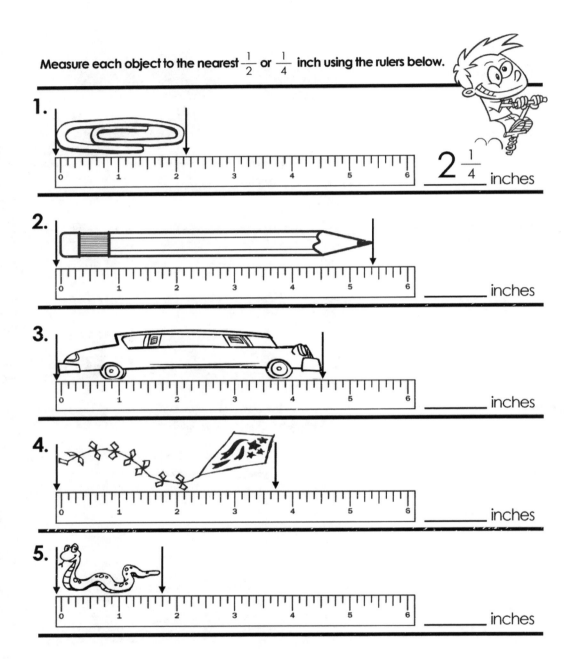

1. $2\frac{1}{4}$ inches

2. _____ inches

3. _____ inches

4. _____ inches

5. _____ inches

54

Copyright © Mometrix Media. You have been licensed one copy of this document for personal use only. Any other reproduction or redistribution is strictly prohibited. All rights reserved.

# LESSON 5

## LIQUID MEASUREMENT

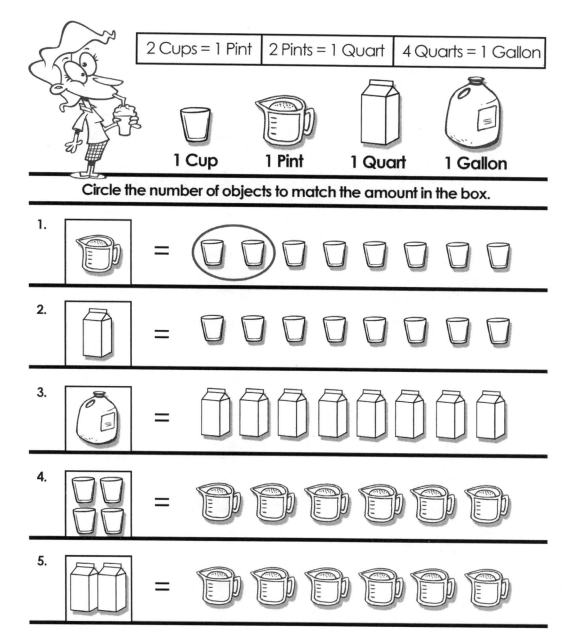

| 2 Cups = 1 Pint | 2 Pints = 1 Quart | 4 Quarts = 1 Gallon |

1 Cup      1 Pint      1 Quart      1 Gallon

Circle the number of objects to match the amount in the box.

1. =

2. =

3. =

4. =

5. =

Copyright © Mometrix Media. You have been licensed one copy of this document for personal use only. Any other reproduction or redistribution is strictly prohibited. All rights reserved.

**CHAPTER 9 - FRACTIONS**

**LESSON 1**

**EXPLAINING FRACTIONS**

A **fraction** names a part of a whole. It can also be used to name a part of a group or set.

Fractions are made up of two parts. The **numerator** and the **denominator**.

$$\frac{1}{4}$$

← The numerator is the number of shaded objects.

← The denominator is the total number of objects.

**Write what fraction of each set is shaded in.**

1. $= \dfrac{1}{3}$

2. $=$

3. $=$

4. $=$

5. $=$

6. $=$

7. $=$

8. $=$

Copyright © Mometrix Media. You have been licensed one copy of this document for personal use only. Any other reproduction or redistribution is strictly prohibited. All rights reserved.

## LESSON 2

## COMPARING FRACTIONS

- These fractions have the same denominators.

- We determine which fraction is larger by looking at the numerator.

- 6 is greater than 5. ( 6 > 5 )

Numerator $\longrightarrow$ $\dfrac{6}{12}$ $\boxed{>}$ $\dfrac{5}{12}$
Denominator $\longrightarrow$

---

### Compare the fractions. Write >, <, or =.

1. $\dfrac{2}{8}$ $\boxed{<}$ $\dfrac{4}{8}$

2. $\dfrac{1}{5}$ $\square$ $\dfrac{4}{5}$

3. $\dfrac{8}{10}$ $\square$ $\dfrac{6}{10}$

4. $\dfrac{2}{3}$ $\square$ $\dfrac{4}{3}$

5. $\dfrac{6}{7}$ $\square$ $\dfrac{2}{7}$

6. $\dfrac{10}{15}$ $\square$ $\dfrac{2}{15}$

7. $\dfrac{2}{6}$ $\square$ $\dfrac{4}{6}$

8. $\dfrac{1}{2}$ $\square$ $\dfrac{2}{2}$

9. $\dfrac{5}{10}$ $\square$ $\dfrac{3}{10}$

10. $\dfrac{3}{8}$ $\square$ $\dfrac{4}{8}$

11. $\dfrac{1}{11}$ $\square$ $\dfrac{9}{11}$

12. $\dfrac{3}{5}$ $\square$ $\dfrac{1}{5}$

13. $\dfrac{1}{3}$ $\square$ $\dfrac{4}{3}$

14. $\dfrac{1}{4}$ $\square$ $\dfrac{3}{4}$

15. $\dfrac{7}{9}$ $\square$ $\dfrac{5}{9}$

Copyright © Mometrix Media. You have been licensed one copy of this document for personal use only. Any other reproduction or redistribution is strictly prohibited. All rights reserved.

## LESSON 3

## ORDERING FRACTIONS

Write these fractions in order from least to greatest.

1.  $1\frac{6}{10}$, $2\frac{3}{10}$, $1\frac{1}{10}$, $2\frac{1}{10}$     $1\frac{1}{10}$, $1\frac{6}{10}$, $2\frac{1}{10}$, $2\frac{3}{10}$

2.  $4\frac{4}{8}$, $9\frac{6}{8}$, $6\frac{2}{8}$, $9\frac{3}{8}$

3.  $6\frac{1}{4}$, $7\frac{1}{4}$, $6\frac{2}{4}$, $7\frac{3}{4}$

4.  $8\frac{1}{9}$, $9\frac{1}{9}$, $8\frac{2}{9}$, $8\frac{3}{9}$

5.  $3\frac{8}{12}$, $3\frac{1}{12}$, $1\frac{1}{12}$, $2\frac{3}{12}$

6.  $5\frac{3}{54}$, $5\frac{2}{54}$, $5\frac{1}{54}$, $5\frac{7}{54}$

Copyright © Mometrix Media. You have been licensed one copy of this document for personal use only. Any other reproduction or redistribution is strictly prohibited. All rights reserved.

## LESSON 4

### ADDING FRACTIONS WITH COMMON DENOMINATORS

To add fractions with common denominators, just add the numerators. The denominators will remain the same.

Numerators ⟶  $\dfrac{2}{9} + \dfrac{3}{9} = \dfrac{2+3}{9} = \dfrac{5}{9}$
Common Denominators ⟶

### Add the fractions below.

1. $\dfrac{1}{5} + \dfrac{3}{5} = \dfrac{4}{5}$

2. $\dfrac{5}{10} + \dfrac{3}{10} = $ _____

3. $\dfrac{3}{6} + \dfrac{2}{6} = $ _____

4. $\dfrac{7}{12} + \dfrac{3}{12} = $ _____

5. $\dfrac{4}{9} + \dfrac{4}{9} = $ _____

6. $\dfrac{6}{14} + \dfrac{2}{14} = $ _____

7. $\dfrac{3}{7} + \dfrac{2}{7} = $ _____

8. $\dfrac{1}{4} + \dfrac{2}{4} = $ _____

9. $\dfrac{2}{6} + \dfrac{3}{6} = $ _____

10. $\dfrac{4}{8} + \dfrac{3}{8} = $ _____

11. $\dfrac{6}{11} + \dfrac{3}{11} = $ _____

12. $\dfrac{7}{15} + \dfrac{5}{15} = $ _____

13. $\dfrac{3}{14} + \dfrac{9}{14} = $ _____

14. $\dfrac{1}{3} + \dfrac{1}{3} = $ _____

15. $\dfrac{2}{8} + \dfrac{4}{8} = $ _____

16. $\dfrac{3}{5} + \dfrac{1}{5} = $ _____

17. $\dfrac{9}{13} + \dfrac{2}{13} = $ _____

18. $\dfrac{1}{10} + \dfrac{6}{10} = $ _____

Copyright © Mometrix Media. You have been licensed one copy of this document for personal use only. Any other reproduction or redistribution is strictly prohibited. All rights reserved.

## LESSON 5

### SUBTRACTING FRACTIONS WITH COMMON DENOMINATORS

To subtract fractions with common denominators, just subtract the numerators. The denominators will remain the same.

| Numerators | $\longrightarrow$ | $\dfrac{9}{10}$ | $-$ | $\dfrac{4}{10}$ | $=$ | $\dfrac{9-4}{10}$ | $=$ | $\dfrac{5}{10}$ |
| Common Denominators | $\longrightarrow$ | | | | | | | |

---

### Subtract the fractions below.

---

**1.** $\dfrac{7}{15} - \dfrac{3}{15} = \dfrac{4}{15}$

**2.** $\dfrac{7}{9} - \dfrac{2}{9} = $ ____

**3.** $\dfrac{12}{14} - \dfrac{7}{14} = $ ____

**4.** $\dfrac{8}{8} - \dfrac{6}{8} = $ ____

**5.** $\dfrac{28}{39} - \dfrac{19}{39} = $ ____

**6.** $\dfrac{24}{39} - \dfrac{11}{39} = $ ____

**7.** $\dfrac{9}{10} - \dfrac{2}{10} = $ ____

**8.** $\dfrac{13}{15} - \dfrac{9}{15} = $ ____

**9.** $\dfrac{13}{16} - \dfrac{3}{16} = $ ____

**10.** $\dfrac{6}{7} - \dfrac{4}{7} = $ ____

**11.** $\dfrac{10}{26} - \dfrac{8}{26} = $ ____

**12.** $\dfrac{60}{62} - \dfrac{41}{62} = $ ____

**13.** $\dfrac{19}{24} - \dfrac{10}{24} = $ ____

**14.** $\dfrac{46}{54} - \dfrac{17}{54} = $ ____

**15.** $\dfrac{98}{98} - \dfrac{15}{98} = $ ____

Copyright © Mometrix Media. You have been licensed one copy of this document for personal use only. Any other reproduction or redistribution is strictly prohibited. All rights reserved.

## LESSON 6

## ADDING MIXED NUMBERS WITH COMMON DENOMINATORS

A **mixed number** is a number written as a whole number and a fraction.

When adding mixed numbers with common denominators, add the whole numbers first, then add the numerators. The denominators will remain the same.

$$1\frac{2}{4} + 5\frac{1}{4} = 6\frac{3}{4} \longleftarrow \text{Numerator}$$
$$\longleftarrow \text{Denominator}$$

### Add the mixed numbers below.

1. $5\frac{3}{8}$
$+3\frac{2}{8}$

$8\frac{5}{8}$

2. $2\frac{2}{5}$
$+1\frac{2}{5}$

3. $9\frac{3}{10}$
$+3\frac{4}{10}$

4. $2\frac{6}{15}$
$+2\frac{4}{15}$

5. $4\frac{9}{21}$
$+5\frac{5}{21}$

6. $7\frac{20}{42}$
$+6\frac{14}{42}$

7. $13\frac{7}{9}$
$+3\frac{1}{9}$

8. $12\frac{6}{29}$
$+11\frac{9}{29}$

61

Copyright © Mometrix Media. You have been licensed one copy of this document for personal use only. Any other reproduction or redistribution is strictly prohibited. All rights reserved.

## LESSON 7

## SUBTRACTING MIXED NUMBERS WITH COMMON DENOMINATORS

A **mixed number** is a number written as a whole number and a fraction.

When subtracting mixed numbers with common denominators, subtract the whole numbers first, then subtract the numerators. The denominators will remain the same.

$$9\frac{5}{6} - 4\frac{2}{6} = 5\frac{3}{6} \longleftarrow \text{Numerator}$$
$$\longleftarrow \text{Denominator}$$

**Subtract the mixed numbers below.**

1.  $6\frac{3}{4}$
    $- 4\frac{1}{4}$
    _____
    $2\frac{2}{4}$

2.  $8\frac{4}{6}$
    $- 3\frac{2}{6}$
    _____

3.  $5\frac{8}{9}$
    $- 2\frac{7}{9}$
    _____

4.  $9\frac{11}{13}$
    $- 8\frac{9}{13}$
    _____

5.  $32\frac{15}{21}$
    $-18\frac{5}{21}$
    _____

6.  $12\frac{7}{30}$
    $- 2\frac{2}{30}$
    _____

7.  $17\frac{20}{26}$
    $-11\frac{12}{26}$
    _____

8.  $25\frac{13}{17}$
    $-18\frac{8}{17}$
    _____

62

Copyright © Mometrix Media. You have been licensed one copy of this document for personal use only. Any other reproduction or redistribution is strictly prohibited. All rights reserved.

## LESSON 8

## REDUCING FRACTIONS

- Reducing (or simplifying) fractions means reducing a fraction to the lowest possible terms.
  - To do this, find a number that both the numerator and the denominator of the fraction are divisible by. Use that number as the numerator and denominator of a new fraction equal to one. Then divide the fractions.

| Example 1: | Example 2: |
|---|---|
| $\dfrac{15}{20} \div \dfrac{5}{5} = \dfrac{3}{4}$ | $\dfrac{3}{9} \div \dfrac{3}{3} = \dfrac{1}{3}$ |
| $\dfrac{15}{20} = \left\lceil \dfrac{3}{4} \right\rceil$ | $\dfrac{3}{9} = \left\lceil \dfrac{1}{3} \right\rceil$ |

### Write the problems out and reduce the fractions below.

**1.** $\dfrac{5}{15} \div \dfrac{3}{3} = \dfrac{1}{3}$

**2.** $\dfrac{4}{12} \div \underline{\quad} = \underline{\quad}$

**3.** $\dfrac{6}{15} \div \underline{\quad} = \underline{\quad}$

**4.** $\dfrac{8}{10} \div \underline{\quad} = \underline{\quad}$

**5.** $\dfrac{10}{25} \div \underline{\quad} = \underline{\quad}$

**6.** $\dfrac{20}{25} \div \underline{\quad} = \underline{\quad}$

Copyright © Mometrix Media. You have been licensed one copy of this document for personal use only. Any other reproduction or redistribution is strictly prohibited. All rights reserved.

# Practice Test #1

## Practice Questions

**1. Which fraction is represented by the diagram shown below?**

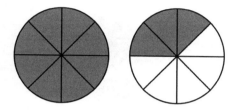

    a.   $1\frac{1}{8}$

    b.   $1\frac{1}{4}$

    c.   $1\frac{3}{8}$

    d.   $1\frac{1}{2}$

**2. Which of the following models represents a fraction equivalent to $\frac{2}{5}$?**

    a.   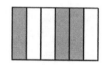          b.   

    c.             d.   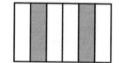

**3. If Hannah drives 1104 miles a month and Carrie drives 1339 miles a month. How many miles do they drive each month combined?**

_____

**4. Jasper collects 1,082 cans of food. He gives a certain number of cans to the first local charity he finds. He now has 602 cans of food. How many cans of food did he give to the first local charity?**

    a.   430

    b.   480

    c.   682

    d.   1,684

Copyright © Mometrix Media. You have been licensed one copy of this document for personal use only. Any other reproduction or redistribution is strictly prohibited. All rights reserved.

**5. Which of the following models represents a fraction less than the fraction shown below?**

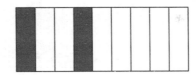

a.
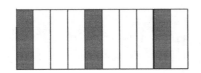

b.
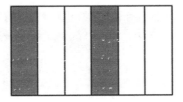

c.
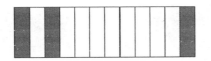

d.
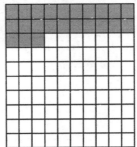

**6. Suppose each flat represents one unit. What number if represented below?**

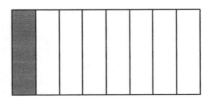

    a.  12.3
    b.  1.23
    c.  0.123
    d.  100.23

**7. Amanda creates the base of a picture frame, using 4.55 inches of red fabric and 6.25 inches of blue fabric. How many inches of fabric are used to create the base of the frame?**

    a.  10.80 inches
    b.  10.85 inches
    c.  10.75 inches
    d.  10.90 inches

Copyright © Mometrix Media. You have been licensed one copy of this document for personal use only. Any other reproduction or redistribution is strictly prohibited. All rights reserved.

8. Travis has a stick that is 5/16 of a meter long, and Steven has a stick that is 7/8 of a meter long. If they lay the sticks end to end how long would they be?

    a.  $\frac{12}{16}$ meter

    b.  $1\frac{3}{16}$

    c.  $1\frac{3}{8}$

    d.  $1\frac{1}{8}$

9. Hannah ran 12 laps every day for 8 days. How many laps did she run in all?

    a.  108
    b.  96
    c.  84
    d.  72

10. Kevin approved 13 trees out of every group of trees he surveyed. He surveyed 15 groups of trees. How many trees did he approve?

    a.  155
    b.  165
    c.  195
    d.  205

11. Monique has $690 to spend on a 3-day trip. She plans to spend an equal amount of money per day. How many dollars can she spend per day?

_____

12. Three friends sold cupcakes for a fundraiser. Eli sold 84 cupcakes, John sold 46 cupcakes, and Kim sold 72 cupcakes. Which of the following is the best estimate for the number of cupcakes the three friends sold in all?

    a.  180
    b.  200
    c.  210
    d.  190

13. Lynn has $316 to spend on groceries for the month. He plans to spend the same amount of money on groceries each week. Which of the following is the best estimate for the amount of money he can spend on groceries each week?

    a.  $65
    b.  $75
    c.  $90
    d.  $95

14. Carlisle charges $21.95 per hair cut and has completed 30 haircuts this week. Which of the following is the best approximation for the total charges for all haircuts?

    a.  $450
    b.  $600
    c.  $750
    d.  $800

Copyright © Mometrix Media. You have been licensed one copy of this document for personal use only. Any other reproduction or redistribution is strictly prohibited. All rights reserved.

15. Which of the following number sentences belongs in the fact family shown below?

$$7 \times 6 = 42$$
$$6 \times 7 = 42$$
$$42 \div 7 = 6$$

   a. $7 + 6 = 13$
   b. $42 \div 6 = 7$
   c. $42 + 7 = 49$
   d. $42 - 6 = 36$

16. Which of the following number sentences is represented by the array shown below?

X X X X X
X X X X X
X X X X X
X X X X X

   a. $4 + 6 = 10$
   b. $4 \times 6 = 24$
   c. $24 - 6 = 18$
   d. $24 \div 3 = 8$

17. Billy is going on vacation. He will travel a total of 1486 miles while he is gone. If Location A is 572 miles away from home and then Location B is 437 miles from location A. How long is the trip from Location B back to home? Explain how you came up with your answer.

_____

_____

_____

18. A door is $7\frac{1}{4}$ feet tall. How many inches is it? Explain the process used to come up with your answer.

_____

_____

_____

19. What is the 8th number in the pattern shown below?

108, 96, 84, 72, ...

   a. 48
   b. 36
   c. 24
   d. 12

Copyright © Mometrix Media. You have been licensed one copy of this document for personal use only. Any other reproduction or redistribution is strictly prohibited. All rights reserved.

**20. Mrs. Thompson writes the number sentences shown below:**

$$100 \times 13 = 1300$$
$$100 \times 14 = 1400$$
$$100 \times 15 = 1500$$
$$100 \times 24 = ?$$

**What is the product of the last number sentence?**

a.  2200
b.  2300
c.  2400
d.  2500

**21. The number of sit-ups Aisha has completed over a period of 3 days is shown in the table below.**

| Day | Number of Sit-ups |
|-----|-------------------|
| 1   | 35                |
| 2   | 70                |
| 3   | 105               |

**If this pattern continues, how many sit-ups will she have completed after 7 days?**

_____

**22. Which of the following correctly describes the relationship between the values of x and y, as shown in the table below?**

| x | y  |
|---|----|
| 1 | 4  |
| 2 | 8  |
| 3 | 12 |
| 4 | 16 |

a.  The value of $x$ is 6 less than the value of $y$
b.  The value of $y$ is 4 times the value of $x$
c.  The value of $y$ is 4 more than the value of $x$
d.  The value of $x$ is 1 less than the value of $y$

**23. If the measure of angle *BAC* is 38° and the measure of angle *DAE* is 49°, then what is the measure of angle *CAD*?**

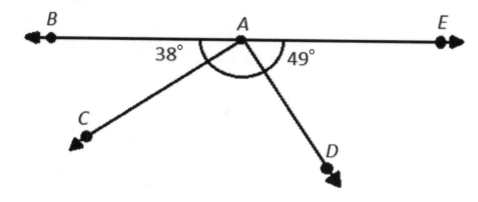

Copyright © Mometrix Media. You have been licensed one copy of this document for personal use only. Any other reproduction or redistribution is strictly prohibited. All rights reserved.

24. A farm has only cows and chickens. There are 5 chicken coops with 14 chickens each, and 6 barns with 16 cows each. How many total animals are on the farm?

    a. 41
    b. 330
    c. 164
    d. 166

25. Which shape has 5 sides?

    a. hexagon
    b. pentagon
    c. octagon
    d. heptagon

26. Given the numbers below, fill in the blank with the correct symbol (<, >, =) to make the statement true.

    4.22 _____ 4.2
    .09 _____ .9
    2.72 _____ 2.702

27. What number is represented by Point A, shown on the number line below?

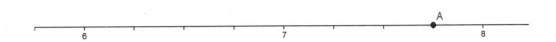

    a. $7\frac{3}{8}$
    b. $7\frac{1}{2}$
    c. $7\frac{1}{4}$
    d. $7\frac{3}{4}$

28. A triangle is rotated about one of its vertices. Which of the following statements is true?

    a. The rotated triangle is similar to, but not congruent to, the original triangle
    b. The rotated triangle is congruent to the original triangle
    c. The rotated triangle is not similar to or congruent to the original triangle
    d. The rotated triangle is larger than the original triangle

29. Which of the following are multiples of 7? Select all that apply.

    I. 7
    II. 21
    III. 27
    IV. 39
    V. 42
    VI. 77

Copyright © Mometrix Media. You have been licensed one copy of this document for personal use only. Any other reproduction or redistribution is strictly prohibited. All rights reserved.

30. Jason walks 2,847 feet to school. Kevin walks 3,128 feet to school. What is the difference in the distance that they walk to school?

31. Ana draws a line with chalk that is $14\frac{5}{8}$ feet long. Then she erases $3\frac{3}{8}$ feet. How long is the line now? Explain why your answer is correct.

32. Which of the following are factors of 42? Select all that apply.
   I. 1 and 42
   II. 2 and 22
   III. 3 and 14
   IV. 4 and 11
   V. 5 and 8
   VI. 6 and 7

33. A box has a length of 7.5 inches, a width of 3.85 inches, and a height of 2.3 inches. Which of the following best represents the volume of the box?
   a. $28 \text{ in}^3$
   b. $36 \text{ in}^3$
   c. $48 \text{ in}^3$
   d. $64 \text{ in}^3$

34. A cafeteria offers 3 meats, 3 vegetables, 2 breads, and 2 desserts. How many possible meal combinations are there? Explain how to find the answer.

35. The average number of miles per hour driven by a sample of drivers is shown below.
65, 70, 60, 55, 70, 65, 70, 60, 65, 70, 55, 65, 70, 55, 60

Based on the data, which average speed is driven by the most drivers?
   a. 55
   b. 60
   c. 65
   d. 70

Copyright © Mometrix Media. You have been licensed one copy of this document for personal use only. Any other reproduction or redistribution is strictly prohibited. All rights reserved.

36. Kelsey surveys her classmates to determine their favorite types of music. The results are shown in the table below.

| Type of Music | Number of Students |
| --- | --- |
| Classical | 7 |
| Rock | 8 |
| Blues | 11 |
| Country | 4 |
| Other | 10 |

**Which circle graph correctly represents the results?**

a.

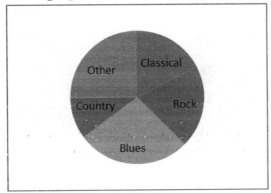

c.

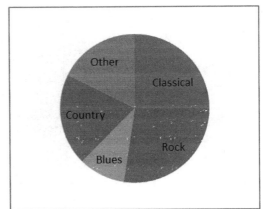

b.

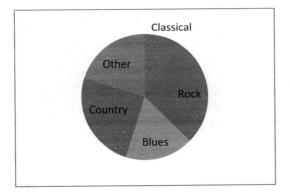

d.

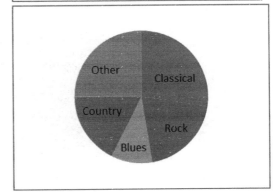

Copyright © Mometrix Media. You have been licensed one copy of this document for personal use only. Any other reproduction or redistribution is strictly prohibited. All rights reserved.

**37. The bar graph below represents student preferences for different parks in Flagstaff, Arizona.**

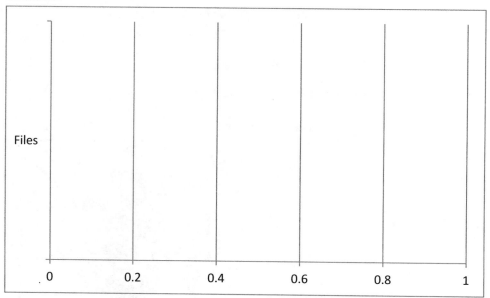

**Which park is preferred by the most students?**

    a.   Bushmaster

    b.   Wheeler

    c.   Oxenglenn

    d.   Forest

Copyright © Mometrix Media. You have been licensed one copy of this document for personal use only. Any other reproduction or redistribution is strictly prohibited. All rights reserved.

# Answers and Explanations

**1. C:** The diagram represents one whole, plus three-eighths of a second whole. Therefore, the diagram represents the fraction, $1\frac{3}{8}$.

**2. B:** The fraction, $\frac{2}{5}$, is equivalent to the fraction, $\frac{4}{10}$. The numerator and denominator of the given fraction are both multiplied by 2 to obtain the model for $\frac{4}{10}$; the fractions are proportional.

**3. 2443:** To find their combined miles just add them together.

**4. B:** In order to find the number of cans of food he gave to the first charity, the number of cans of food he has left needs to be subtracted from the number of cans he collected; $1,082 - 602 = 480$.

**5. B:** The given model represents the fraction, $\frac{2}{9}$, which is approximately 0.22. The model for Choice B represents the fraction, $\frac{1}{8}$, which equals 0.125. This fraction is less than the given fraction. The fractions can also be compared by finding a least common denominator.

**6. B:** Since each flat represents one unit, the first flat represents 1, whereas the second flat represents $\frac{23}{100}$, or 0.23. Together, the diagram represents the number, 1.23.

**7. A:** The sum of the two decimals is 10.80; the decimals are added just like whole numbers are, while aligning the decimal point.

**8. B:** If they lay the sticks end to end then you would just add the lengths together. First convert $\frac{7}{8}$ to $\frac{14}{16}$ then add that to $\frac{5}{16}$ to get $1\frac{3}{16}$.

**9. B:** She runs $12 \times 8$ laps in all, or 96 laps.

**10. C:** Since he approved 13 trees out of every group of trees and surveyed 15 groups, he approved $13 \times 15$ trees, or 195 trees.

**11. 230:** In order to find the amount of money she can spend each day, 690 should be divided by 3; $690 \div 3 = 230$. Thus, she can spend 230 dollars per day.

**12. B:** The number of cupcakes sold can be rounded as follows: 80 cupcakes, 50 cupcakes, and 70 cupcakes, which sum to 200. Therefore, the best estimate for the number of cupcakes sold is 200 cupcakes.

**13. B:** The amount of money Lynn has to spend on groceries for the month can be rounded to $300; $300 \div 4 = 75$. Thus, the best estimate for the amount of money he can spend per week is $75.

**14. B:** The amount of money Carlisle charges per hair cut can be rounded to $20; $20 \times 30 = 600$. Thus, his total charges are approximately $600.

**15. B:** The missing number sentence in the fact family is the other division number sentence, which reads: $42 \div 6 = 7$.

**16. B:** The array represents the multiplication sentence, $4 \times 6 = 24$. Note. There are 4 rows and 6 x's in each row.

Copyright © Mometrix Media. You have been licensed one copy of this document for personal use only. Any other reproduction or redistribution is strictly prohibited. All rights reserved.

**17. 477:** If he travels 572 miles and then 437 miles then he only has 477 miles left to go. 1486-572-437=477.

**18. 87 in.:** There are 12 inches in a foot. $12 \times 7 = 84$. Then divide 12 by 4 to get 3. 84+3=87.

**19. C:** The pattern represents a sequence that subtracts 12 from each previous term. The first number in the pattern represents the product of 9 and 12; $9 \times 12 = 108$. The eighth number in the pattern is 7 numbers away from the first number of 108. Thus, the eighth number represents the product of 2 and 12, which equals 24. The eighth number in the pattern is 24. The eighth number in the pattern can also be found by subtracting 12 from the last given number in the pattern 4 more times; $72 - 12 = 60$; $60 - 12 = 48$; $48 - 12 = 36$; $36 - 12 = 24$.

**20. C:** As noted in the pattern, the product of 100 and 24 can be found by multiplying 24 by 1 and adding two zeros to the product. Thus, the product of 100 and 24 is 2400.

**21. 245.** Since she completes 35 each day, she has completed $35 \times 7$ situps after 7 days; $35 \times 7 = 245$.

**22. B:** The value of y is indeed 4 times the value of x. Note. 4 is 4 times the value of 1; 8 is 4 times the value of 2; 12 is 4 times the value of 3; and 16 is 4 times the value of 4.

**23. 93°:** Since the angle of a straight line is known to be 180°, then 38° *and* 49° can be subtracted from that to get 93°.

**24. D:** Multiply the 5 chicken coops times the 14 chickens to get 70. Then multiply the 6 barns times the 16 cows to get 96. Add those together to get 166.

**25. B:** A pentagon has 5 sides.

**26.** $4.22 > 4.2$

$.09 < .9$

$2.72 > 2.702$

**27. D:** The number line is divided into fourths. Thus, between the whole numbers, 7 and 8, lie the fractions, $7\frac{1}{4}, 7\frac{2}{4}$, and $7\frac{3}{4}$. Point A represents the fraction, $7\frac{3}{4}$.

**28. D:** To multiply a whole number by a fraction, multiply the whole number by the numerator only to receive the product. When multiplying 16 by 1/5th, multiply 16 by 1, and leave the denominator as 5. The product is 16/5. Similarly, when multiplying 4 by 4/5, the product is 16/5.

**29. I,II,V,VI:** $7 \times 1 = 1, 7 \times 3 = 21, 7 \times 6 = 42, 7 \times 11 = 77$

**30. 281:** To find the difference just subtract. 3128-2847=281

**31. $11\frac{1}{4}$:** To find the length just subtract $3\frac{3}{8}$ from $14\frac{5}{8}$.

**32. I, III, VI:** $1 \times 42 = 42, 3 \times 14 = 42, 6 \times 7 = 42$

**33. D:** The measurements of the box can be rounded to 8 inches, 4 inches, and 2 inches. The volume of the box is equal to the product of the measurements of the length, width, and height of the box. Thus, the volume is approximately $8 \times 4 \times 2$, or 64 cubic inches.

Copyright © Mometrix Media. You have been licensed one copy of this document for personal use only. Any other reproduction or redistribution is strictly prohibited. All rights reserved.

**34. 36.** The possible meal combinations are equal to the product of the number of different types of each part of the meal. Thus, the possible meal combinations are equal to $3 \times 3 \times 2 \times 2$, or 36.

**35. D:** Five drivers drove at an average speed of 70 miles per hour, which is more than any other number of drivers, driving at a particular speed; three drivers drove at an average speed of 55 miles per hour, three drivers drove at an average speed of 60 miles per hour, and four drivers drove at an average speed of 65 miles per hour.

**36. A:** The circle graph can be created by determining the fraction of students, with preferences for each type of music. The total number of students surveyed is 40. Thus, 7 out of 40 students, or $\frac{7}{40}$ students, prefer classical music; 8 out of 40 students, or $\frac{8}{40}$ students, prefer rock music; 11 out of 40 students, or $\frac{11}{40}$ students, prefer blues; 4 out of 40 students, or $\frac{4}{40}$ students, prefer country; and 10 out of 40 students, or $\frac{10}{40}$ students, prefer other music. These fractions can be converted to the following percentages: approximately 18% prefer classical music, 20% prefer rock music, approximately 28% prefer blues, 10% prefer country, and 25% prefer other music. The circle graph, shown for Choice A, correctly represents these percentages.

**37. A:** There were 9 students who preferred Bushmaster Park; 9 students is more than any other number of students displayed on the bar graph.

Copyright © Mometrix Media. You have been licensed one copy of this document for personal use only. Any other reproduction or redistribution is strictly prohibited. All rights reserved.

# Practice Test #2

## Practice Questions

1. A room has 6 rows of 9 chairs. The room next to it has 32 chairs. Together how many chairs do they have?

    a.  54
    b.  56
    c.  86
    d.  84

2. Amanda buys a sandwich and pays the amount of money shown below. How much does she pay?

    a.  $3.56
    b.  $3.61
    c.  $3.50
    d.  $3.51

3. Which of the following sets represents a fraction equivalent to $\frac{8}{12}$?

    a.

    b.

    c.

    d.

76

Copyright © Mometrix Media. You have been licensed one copy of this document for personal use only. Any other reproduction or redistribution is strictly prohibited. All rights reserved.

4. Which fraction is represented by the diagram shown below?

a. $1\frac{1}{2}$

b. $1\frac{2}{5}$

c. $1\frac{3}{5}$

d. $1\frac{3}{4}$

5. Which of the following fractions are equal to $\frac{2}{3}$? Select all that apply.

I. $\frac{1}{6}$

II. $\frac{6}{9}$

III. $\frac{4}{6}$

IV. $\frac{5}{8}$

V. $\frac{6}{10}$

6. Martin saved $156 in September, $173 in October, and $219 in November. How much money did he save during the three months?

a. $538

b. $569

c. $548

d. $576

7. Andrea pays $120 more in rent per month this year than she did last year. She pays $763 per month this year. How much did she pay per month last year?

a. $663

b. $643

c. $863

d. $883

8. Which sum is represented by the diagram shown below?

 +

a. 1.08

b. 1.09

c. 1.10

d. 1.11

Copyright © Mometrix Media. You have been licensed one copy of this document for personal use only. Any other reproduction or redistribution is strictly prohibited. All rights reserved.

**9. Which fact is represented by the array shown below?**

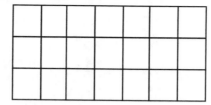

    a.   $3 + 7 = 10$
    b.   $21 - 7 = 14$
    c.   $3 \times 7 = 21$
    d.   $10 + 7 = 17$

**10. A candle-making shop sold 18 candles on Friday, 37 candles on Saturday, and 23 candles on Sunday. Which of the following is the best estimate for the number of candles sold during the three days?**

    a.   60
    b.   70
    c.   80
    d.   90

**11. Isabelle must drive 1,482 miles. She plans to drive approximately the same number of miles per day over the period of 5 days. Which of the following is the best approximation for the number of miles she will drive per day? Explain how you approximated your answer.**

    a.   250
    b.   300
    c.   350
    d.   400

_____

_____

_____

**12. Mr. Jacobsen buys 32 boxes of oatmeal. Each box contains 20 packets of oatmeal. How many total packets of oatmeal did he buy? Explain why your answer is correct?**

_____

_____

_____

Copyright © Mometrix Media. You have been licensed one copy of this document for personal use only. Any other reproduction or redistribution is strictly prohibited. All rights reserved.

**13.** Mr. Johnson ordered 1 pizza for every 3 kids in his class. If he ordered 7 pizzas then how many kids does he have in his class?

_____

**14.** Eli has 42 crayons and plans to give the same number of crayons to each of his 6 friends. Which number sentence can be used to find the number of crayons he will give to each friend?

    a.   $42 - 6 = 36$
    b.   $42 \div 6 = 7$
    c.   $42 \times 6 = 252$
    d.   $42 + 6 = 48$

**15. Part A:** What fraction does the shaded area of the cirle below represent?

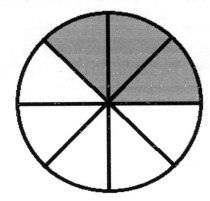

    a.   $\frac{2}{3}$
    b.   $\frac{3}{6}$
    c.   $\frac{3}{8}$
    d.   $\frac{1}{3}$

**Part B:** If 3 more slices of the circle are shaded in then what fraction would it be?

    a.   $\frac{5}{8}$
    b.   $\frac{5}{6}$
    c.   $\frac{2}{3}$
    d.   $\frac{3}{4}$

Copyright © Mometrix Media. You have been licensed one copy of this document for personal use only. Any other reproduction or redistribution is strictly prohibited. All rights reserved.

16. The number of miles Brad has driven over a period of 3 days is shown in the table below.

| Day | Number of Miles |
|-----|-----------------|
| 1   | 275             |
| 2   | 550             |
| 3   | 825             |

If this pattern continues, how many miles will he have driven after 8 days?

    a. 2,000
    b. 2,025
    c. 2,075
    d. 2,200

17. A local citizen represents the total amount she has donated to a charity over the course of five years, using the table shown below.

| Year | 1 | 2 | 3 | 4 | 5 |
|------|------|------|------|------|------|
| Amount Donated | $250 | $550 | $850 | $1,150 | $1,450 |

If this pattern continues, how much will she have donated after 10 years?

    a. $2,850
    b. $2,900
    c. $2,950
    d. $3,000

18. Jenny will be in a parade and will be throwing out candy. She has 20 pieces of candy, but she thinks that she will need 12 times that much since the parade is so long. How many pieces does she think she needs? Explain how you came up with this answer.

_____

_____

_____

19. Morris needs to define an obtuse angle. Which of the following correctly describes the requirements for such an angle?

    a. An angle with a measure greater than 180 degrees
    b. An angle with a measure greater than 120 degrees
    c. An angle with a measure less than 90 degrees
    d. An angle with a measure greater than 90 degrees

20. If John works 386 minutes a day, how many minutes does he work in a 5 day work week?

_____

Copyright © Mometrix Media. You have been licensed one copy of this document for personal use only. Any other reproduction or redistribution is strictly prohibited. All rights reserved.

21. Benjamin was given a homework problem by his math teacher. He answered the problem by saying that $2.21 + 3.33 = 5.54$, because $2 + 3 = 5$ and $21 + 33 = 54$. He then adds his answer to 4.77 to get 9.131, because $4 + 5 = 9$ and $54 + 77 = 131$. Explain what is wrong with Benjamin's reasoning and how to fix it.

22. Sally eats $\frac{1}{4}$ of a pie, Jesse eats $\frac{1}{8}$ of the same pie, and Lisa eats $\frac{3}{8}$ of the pie. How much of the pie is left? Explain how you came up with your answer.

a. $\frac{1}{4}$

b. $\frac{3}{8}$

c. $\frac{1}{8}$

d. $\frac{1}{2}$

23. Part A: Which of the following figures does not have any parallel sides?

a.

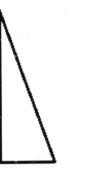

b.

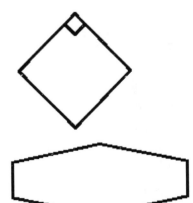

c.

d.

Copyright © Mometrix Media. You have been licensed one copy of this document for personal use only. Any other reproduction or redistribution is strictly prohibited. All rights reserved.

**Part B: Which one does not have any perpendicular sides?**
   a. Figure A
   b. Figure B
   c. Figure C
   d. Figure D

## 24. Which of the following figures has 5 vertices?
   a. triangular prism
   b. square pyramid
   c. rectangular prism
   d. triangular pyramid

## 25. What decimal is represented by Point P, shown on the number line below?

   a. 5.6
   b. 5.7
   c. 5.8
   d. 5.9

## 26. What Point represents $3\frac{3}{4}$, on the number line below?

   a. Point A
   b. Point B
   c. Point C
   d. Point D

Copyright © Mometrix Media. You have been licensed one copy of this document for personal use only. Any other reproduction or redistribution is strictly prohibited. All rights reserved.

27. Triangle ABC is translated as shown below.

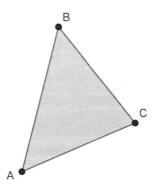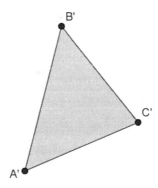

**Which of the following correctly describes the two triangles?**
    a.   The translated triangle is not similar to or congruent to the original triangle.
    b.   The translated triangle has been stretched.
    c.   The translated triangle is congruent to the original triangle.
    d.   The translated triangle is similar to, but not congruent to, the original triangle.

**28. A school has 14 classrooms. Each classroom has 22 students in it. How many total students are in the school?**
    a.   36
    b.   288
    c.   304
    d.   308

**29. Part A: A teacher took a survey of 4th, 5th, and 6th grade students about their favorite animals. Based on the results below how many total students were surveyed?**

|  | Cat | Dog | Fish | Bird |
|---|---|---|---|---|
| 4th Grade | 8 | 10 | 5 | 4 |
| 5th Grade | 10 | 12 | 4 | 4 |
| 6th Grade | 7 | 13 | 2 | 3 |

**Part B: What fraction of 5th grade students chose cats as their favorite animal?**
    a.   $\dfrac{2}{3}$
    b.   $\dfrac{1}{3}$
    c.   $\dfrac{12}{30}$
    d.   $\dfrac{10}{28}$

Copyright © Mometrix Media. You have been licensed one copy of this document for personal use only. Any other reproduction or redistribution is strictly prohibited. All rights reserved.

**30. Given the number 2,573. The number 5 is in what place?**

    a.  ones
    b.  tens
    c.  hundreds
    d.  thousands

**31. In the rectangle below each small square is one square unit. How many square units make up the area of the entire rectangle?**

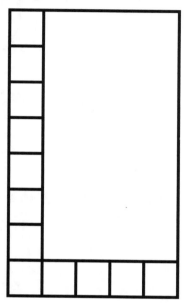

    a.  28
    b.  40
    c.  12
    d.  35

**32. If Kara has 24 hair pins and she buys 6 more packages that each contain 12 hair pins. How many hair pins does she have now?**

**33. A gift box has a length of 18 inches, a width of 12 inches, and a height of 8 inches. Which of the following is the best estimate for the volume of the box?**

    a.  2,400 in$^3$
    b.  2,000 in$^3$
    c.  1,200 in$^3$
    d.  2,800 in$^3$

Copyright © Mometrix Media. You have been licensed one copy of this document for personal use only. Any other reproduction or redistribution is strictly prohibited. All rights reserved.

**34. Andy surveys his classmates to determine their favorite season of the year. The results are shown in the table below.**

| Season | Number of Students |
|--------|-------------------|
| Fall | 7 |
| Winter | 3 |
| Spring | 12 |
| Summer | 18 |

**Which circle graph correctly represents the results?**

a.

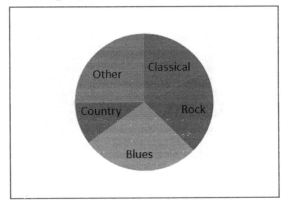

b.

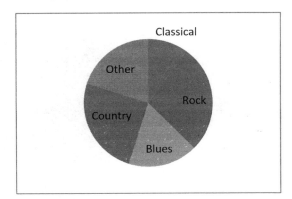

c.

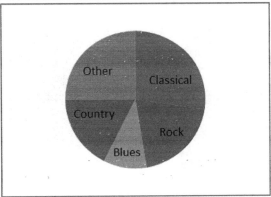

d.

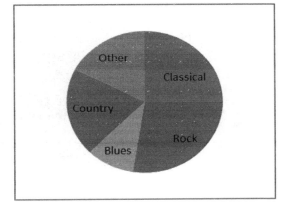

85

Copyright © Mometrix Media. You have been licensed one copy of this document for personal use only. Any other reproduction or redistribution is strictly prohibited. All rights reserved.

35. The bar graph below represents teacher preferences for different vacation states.

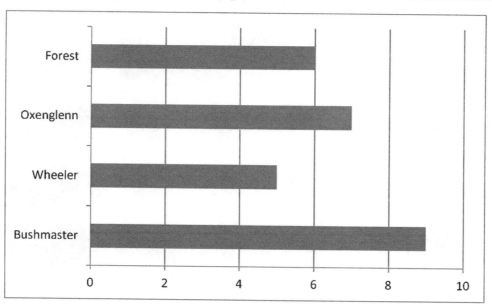

**Which state was preferred by the fewest number of teachers?**
   a. Virginia
   b. Arizona
   c. Texas
   d. New York

36. Alana can choose from 2 shirts, 2 pairs of jeans, 3 pairs of socks, and 2 pairs of shoes. How many possible outfit combinations can she make?

_____

37. The scores on Mrs. Rodriguez's math test are shown below.

95, 78, 92, 99, 74, 83, 89, 92, 79, 85, 87, 90, 88, 92, 79

**Which test score was received by the most students?**
   a. 78
   b. 90
   c. 92
   d. 79

Copyright © Mometrix Media. You have been licensed one copy of this document for personal use only. Any other reproduction or redistribution is strictly prohibited. All rights reserved.

# Answers and Explanations

**1. C:** The first room contains, $6 \times 9 = 54$, chairs. The second contains 32. $54 + 32 = 86$.

**2. D:** The amount of money she pays is equal to the sum of 3 dollar bills, or \$3, and 51 cents, or \$0.51. Thus, she paid \$3.51 for the sandwich.

**3. B:** The fraction, $\frac{8}{12}$, is equivalent to the fraction, $\frac{2}{3}$. The numerator and denominator of the given fraction are both divided by 4 to obtain the model for $\frac{2}{3}$; the fractions are proportional.

**4. B:** The first diagram represents 1 whole, while the second diagram represents $\frac{2}{5}$. Thus the diagram represents $1\frac{2}{5}$, in its entirety.

**5. II, III:** $\frac{4}{6}$ and $\frac{6}{9}$ can both be reduced to $\frac{2}{3}$. This means they are equivalent.

**6. C:** The sum of the dollar amounts is equal to $\$156 + \$173 + \$219$, or \$548.

**7. B:** Since Andrea paid \$120 per month more last year, the amount she paid per month last year is equal to the difference of \$763 and \$120, or \$643.

**8. C:** The diagram represents the sum of $\frac{3}{10}$ and $\frac{8}{10}$, or $\frac{11}{10}$, which is equivalent to $1\frac{1}{10}$, or 1.10. The decimals, $0.30 + 0.80$, can also be added, which equal 1.10.

**9. C:** The array includes 3 rows and 7 columns. Thus, the array represents the number sentence, $3 \times 7 = 21$.

**10. C:** The number of candles sold can be rounded as follows: 20 candles, 40 candles, and 20 candles. Thus, a good estimate of the number of candles sold is $20 + 40 + 20$ candles, or 80 candles.

**11. B:** The distance Isabelle drives can be rounded to 1,500 miles; 1,500 miles divided by 5 days is equal to 300 miles driven per day.

**12. 640:** Each box contains 20 packets, so that's the same as $32 \times 20$, which is 640.

**13. 21:** If 1 pizza feeds 3 people then you can multiply 7 times 3 to figure out that 7 pizzas feeds 21 people.

**14. B:** Since Eli will equally share his crayons, he will divide 42 crayons into 6 groups; $42 \div 6 = 7$.

**15. Part A: C:** The circle is divided into eighths and then 3 of them are shaded.

**Part B: D:** If you shaded 3 more of the eighths that would make $\frac{6}{8}$ which reduces to $\frac{3}{4}$.

**16. D:** Brad drives 275 miles each day. Thus, the total number of miles driven, over a period of days, can be found by adding 275 miles to the number of total miles driven for each previous day. In other words, after 4 days, he drove 1,100 miles. After 5 days, he drove 1,375 miles. After 6 days, he drove 1,650 miles. After 7 days, he drove 1,925 miles. After 8 days, he drove 2,200 miles.

**17. C:** The total amount of money donated is \$300 more each additional year. Thus, the total amount donated, over a period of years, can be found by adding 300 dollars to the amount donated for each previous year. In other words, after 6 years, the total amount donated was \$1,750. After 7

Copyright © Mometrix Media. You have been licensed one copy of this document for personal use only. Any other reproduction or redistribution is strictly prohibited. All rights reserved.

years, the total amount donated was $2,050. After 8 years, the total amount donated was $2,350. After 9 years, the total amount donated was $2,650. After 10 years, the total amount donated was $2,950.

**15. C:** The total amount of money donated is $300 more each additional year. Thus, the total amount donated, over a period of years, can be found by adding 300 dollars to the amount donated for each previous year. In other words, after 6 years, the total amount donated was $1,750. After 7 years, the total amount donated was $2,050. After 8 years, the total amount donated was $2,350. After 9 years, the total amount donated was $2,650. After 10 years, the total amount donated was $2,950.

**19. D:** An obtuse angle has a measure greater than 90 degrees. It may be greater than 120 degrees, but that is not a requirement.

**20. 1930:** To find the answer multiply 386 times 5.

**18. A:** An acute angle is less than 90°. Answer A id the only angle less than 90°.

**22. A:** First add all of the fractions together to find out how much of the pie was eaten. $\frac{1}{4} + \frac{1}{8} + \frac{3}{8} = \frac{6}{8} = \frac{3}{4}$, so that leaves $\frac{1}{4}$ of the pie that was not eaten.

**23. Part A: B:** A triangle does not have any parallel sides.

**Part B: D:** Perpendicular lines always form a 90° angle. None of the sides of a hexagon form a 90° angle.

**24. B:** A square pyramid has 5 vertices, with 4 at the base of the pyramid and 1 at the top.

**25. C:** The number line is divided into tenths. Thus, between the whole numbers, 5 and 6, lie the decimals, 5.1, 5.2, 5.3, 5.4, 5.5, 5.6, 5.7, 5.8, and 5.9. Point P represents the decimal, 5.8.

**26. C:** The number line is divided into fourths. Thus, between the whole numbers, 3 and 4, lie the fractions, $3\frac{1}{4}$, $3\frac{2}{4}$, and $3\frac{3}{4}$. Point C represents the fraction, $3\frac{3}{4}$.

**27. C:** A translated figure is always congruent to the original figure because the size, shape, and angle measures do not change. A translation is simply a slide up, down, right, or left, or a combination of these slides.

**28. D:** To find the answer just multiply 14 times 22.

**29. Part A: 82:** To find the answer add up all of the numbers in the table. This gives the total number of students surveyed.

**Part B: B:** There are 10 5th graders that chose cats as their favorite. There are 30 5th graders total. $\frac{10}{30} = \frac{3}{10}$.

**30. C:** The 2 is in the thousands place. The 5 is in the hundreds place. The 7 is in the tens place, and the 3 is in the ones place.

**31. B:** 8 units make up the length and 5 units make up the width. Area is length times width, so $8 \times 5 = 40$.

88

Copyright © Mometrix Media. You have been licensed one copy of this document for personal use only. Any other reproduction or redistribution is strictly prohibited. All rights reserved.

**32. 96:** If she buys 6 packages of 12 then she buys, 6 × 12 = 72. She already had 24, so 72+24=96.

**33. B:** The dimensions of the box round to 20 inches, 10 inches, and 10 inches. The volume of a box can be determined by finding the product of the dimensions. Thus, the approximate volume is equal to 20 × 10 × 10, or 2,000 cubic inches.

**34. B:** The circle graph can be created by determining the fraction of students, with preferences for each season. The total number of students surveyed is 40. Thus, 7 out of 40 students, or $\frac{7}{40}$ students, prefer Fall; 3 out of 40 students, or $\frac{3}{40}$ students, prefer Winter; 12 out of 40 students, or $\frac{12}{40}$ students, prefer Spring; and 18 out of 40 students, or $\frac{18}{40}$ students, prefer Summer. These fractions can be converted to the following percentages: approximately 18% prefer Fall, approximately 8% prefer Winter, 30% prefer Spring, and 45% prefer Summer. The circle graph, shown for Choice B, correctly represents these percentages.

**35. A:** There were 4 teachers who preferred Virginia; 4 teachers is less than any other number of teachers displayed on the bar graph.

**36. 24.** The possible outfit combinations are equal to the product of the number of different types of each clothing piece. Thus, the possible outfit combinations are equal to 2 × 2 × 3 × 2, or 24.

**37. C:** The score of 92 was received by 3 students, which is more than any other score received; 78 was received by 1 student; 90 was received by 1 student; and 79 was received by 2 students.

Copyright © Mometrix Media. You have been licensed one copy of this document for personal use only. Any other reproduction or redistribution is strictly prohibited. All rights reserved.

# Science

## SCIENTIFIC METHOD

The Steps of the Scientific Method

1. Find a topic to study or investigate. Usually this is in the form of a question. For example, do plants grow better with fertilizer?
2. Gather information about the topic. Read books or search for information on the Internet. Ask an expert in the field. Narrow the broad topic into a specific topic. For example, what is the effect of nitrogen fertilizer on the growth of bean plants?
3. Form a hypothesis or sensible guess that answers the question. Try to answer the question based on what was learned from the research. For example, I think that plants will grow the tallest using the amount of nitrogen fertilizer that is recommended by the manufacturer.
4. Design and perform an experiment to test the hypothesis. An experiment has an independent variable, dependent variable, several constants, and a control if possible. For example, the type of containers, soil, and plants as well as the amount of water and sunlight are the same for every trial of the experiment. Only the concentration of the fertilizer varies or changes.
5. Record the data during the experiment. Then study or analyze the data to determine the relationship between the independent variable and the dependent variable. This usually includes tables, charts, and graphs.
6. State the conclusion. Do the results support or contradict the original hypothesis?

## PURPOSE AND DESIGN OF A GOOD EXPERIMENT

An experiment tests the hypothesis to discover if the hypothesis is true or false. An experiment includes an independent variable, a dependent variable, a control, and several constants. The independent variable is the factor that is changed or varied during the experiment. The dependent variable is the factor that is measured during the experiment. For example, for the hypothesis, ""If bean plants receive the recommended amount of nitrogen fertilizer, then the plants will grow the tallest," the independent variable is the concentration of nitrogen in the fertilizer. The dependent variable is the height of the plant. The control is part of the experiment in which there is no independent variable. The control is used for comparison. For example, the control is a group of plants that receives no fertilizer. The constants are factors that remain the same for all trials of the experiment, including the control. For example, constants include the amount of sunlight and the types of soil, container, and seeds.

### EXAMPLE

Describe an experiment to test the hypothesis, "If bean plants receive the recommended amount of nitrogen fertilizer, then the plants will grow the tallest."

Hypothesis - If bean plants receive the recommended amount of nitrogen fertilizer, then the plants will grow the tallest.

Experiment - The independent variable is the concentration of the fertilizer. The dependent variable is the height of the bean seedlings. The control is a group of seedlings that receive no fertilizer. The constants include the type of pot, soil, bean seedlings, temperature, humidity, and the amount of water and sunlight. Forty seedlings are divided into four groups of ten. Group 1 (the control group) receives no fertilizer. Group 2 receives half of the fertilizer recommended by the manufacturer. Group 3 receives the exact amount recommended by the manufacturer. Group 4

Copyright © Mometrix Media. You have been licensed one copy of this document for personal use only. Any other reproduction or redistribution is strictly prohibited. All rights reserved.

received twice the fertilizer recommended by the manufacturer. The heights of the plants are recorded every three days for six weeks.

## ACT ASPIRE REASONING TEST
### TIPS FOR TAKING THE ACT ASPIRE REASONING TEST

1. ***Don't be scared by science terms or big words.*** For many of the passages, you might not need to completely understand what is written in the paragraphs. Many of the questions are based only on your ability to read and take information from the graphs, charts, tables, figures, or illustrations. New words or difficult words are usually defined.
2. ***The easiest questions usually come right after the passages.*** After quickly reading the passage and skimming the charts or illustrations, see if you can answer the first question from each passage.
3. ***Keep moving.*** Don't spend more than one minute on any question. Keep moving. The easy questions are worth as many points as the harder questions. By spending too much time on the harder questions, you will miss the chance to gain points by answering the easy questions associated with passages you will never even read before the time is up.
4. ***Work on the type of passages you think are the easiest first.*** Be prepared. Know the types of passages and questions covered on this test. Read the passages you feel the most comfortable with first.
5. ***Look for patterns or trends.*** When you read through the passage and glance over the charts and figures, look for patterns or trends. As one variable increases, does the other variable increase or decrease? How does changing one factor affect another factor?

### TOPICS AND THE TYPES OF PASSAGES COVERED ON THE ACT ASPIRE SCIENCE REASONING TEST

The ACT Aspire Science Reasoning Test covers a variety of science topics, including biology such as information about what affects the growth of plants, chemistry such as the pH scale, physics such as the effects of forces on motion, geology such as the different types of minerals, and astronomy such as information about the planets. Students are not expected to know specific or detailed knowledge of each topic. Instead, this test is designed to test your ability to read a scientific passage and find information from the charts, tables, graphs, and illustrations provided with the passage. Difficult terms are usually defined in the passage. Formulas are usually provided.

The ACT Aspire Science Reasoning Test includes three types of passages: data representation, research summaries, and conflicting viewpoints. In the data representation passages, a paragraph with charts, tables, figures, or illustrations is provided about a specific science topic. Students are expected to understand the passage and interpret the information in the charts, graphs, and other visual representations. In the research summary passages, details regarding an experiment and the data from that experiment are provided. Students need to understand, analyze, and interpret graphs and tables. Students need to understand the design of the experiment and interpret the results of the experiment. Students may be asked to make predictions. In the conflicting viewpoint passages, two or more opinions are presented about a scientific topic. Students need to recognize similarities and differences between the viewpoints.

## ACT ASPIRE SCIENCE REASONING TEST
### TYPES OF QUESTIONS ON THE ACT ASPIRE SCIENCE REASONING TEST

Each passage contains a paragraph and usually charts, tables, graphs, illustrations, or figures. This test is designed to test your ability to understand and use the information that is presented in the graphs and charts. To answer a question, you may simply need to read a term from a table or read data from a graph. The more difficult questions may ask for you to recognize patterns or trends. You may need to combine information from the graphs and charts in order to answer a question.

Copyright © Mometrix Media. You have been licensed one copy of this document for personal use only. Any other reproduction or redistribution is strictly prohibited. All rights reserved.

Complex math calculations are not required. Usually you can use estimation to get a close answer and then select from the answers provided in the answer choices. You may have to draw inferences for graphs and figures or interpret coordinating tables.

### STRATEGIES FOR APPROACHING THE DATA REPRESENTATION PASSAGES

#### TIPS FOR THE DATA REPRESENTATION PASSAGES

1. ***Don't be afraid of science passages.*** You don't have to completely understand the passages to answer the questions. Even if the terms and concepts seem hard, the questions are usually pretty easy.
2. ***Usually the easiest questions are first***. After quickly reading the passage and skimming the charts or illustrations, see if you can answer the first question associated with each passage. Usually the easiest questions are first.
3. ***Keep moving!*** Don't spend more than one minute on any particular question. If you don't know the answer, guess and move on. By spending too much time on the harder questions, you will miss the opportunity to gain points by answering the easy questions associated with passages you will never reach before the time is up.
4. ***Problem-solving tips:*** Restate the problem in your own words. Ask yourself what information is needed. Find the information you need to answer the question.
5. ***Pattern, patterns, patterns.*** When you read through the passage and glance over the charts and figures, look for patterns or trends. Do two factors increase? Do two factors decrease? Does one factor increase while a different factor decreases?
6. ***Stick with the information in the passage.*** Don't use any outside science knowledge in answering the actual question. This science knowledge may help you understand the passage, but all the answers should be in the passage or inferred from the passage.

### EXAMPLE

*Partial Passage:* A magnet pulls on objects made of iron or other specific metals. The magnet has a magnetic field that is shown by the field lines in Figure 1. The actual field lines are invisible, but small pieces of iron called iron filings line up in paths resembling the field lines when sprinkled near the magnet. The magnetic field lines follow the path shown by the arrows. The south pole of the magnet is marked with the *S*. The north pole of the magnet is marked with the *N*.

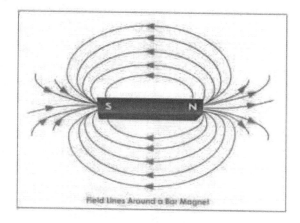

Field Lines Around a Bar Magnet

Figure 1

Copyright © Mometrix Media. You have been licensed one copy of this document for personal use only. Any other reproduction or redistribution is strictly prohibited. All rights reserved.

*Question:* **Which of the following best describes the pattern of tiny iron filings sprinkled near a bar magnet?**

a. Loops drawn from the north pole to the south pole
b. Straight lines drawn towards the magnet from every direction
c. Circles drawn around the magnet but not touching the magnet
d. Waves drawn back and forth between the north and south pole

*Suggested Approach*: According to Figure 1, the arrows on the field lines connected to the north pole are pointing away from the north pole. The arrows on the field lines connected to the south pole are pointing towards the south pole. Iron filings line up with the magnetic field line, which form loops from the north pole to the south pole. Therefore, choice A is correct.

## EXAMPLE

*Partial Passage:* The skin is the largest organ of the body. The skin is made up of three layers.  The top layer is called the epidermis. The epidermis is made up of dead cells. The second layer of skin is called the dermis. The dermis is made up of live cells. Sweat glands and oil glands are located in the dermis. The third layer of the skin is called the subcutaneous layer. The subcutaneous layer helps to connect the skin to the muscle tissue underneath. See Figure 1.

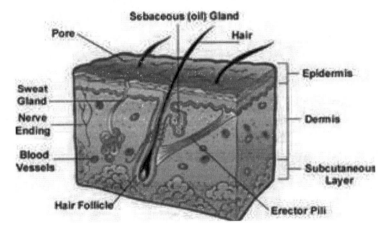

Figure 1

*Question:* **Which of the following lists the layers of the skin from outside of the skin to the inside of the skin?**

a. Dermis, subcutaneous layer, epidermis
b. Epidermis, dermis, subcutaneous layer
c. Subcutaneous layer, epidermis, dermis
d. Epidermis, subcutaneous layer, dermis

*Suggested Approach*: The passage states the top layer of skin is the epidermis. The second layer of skin is the dermis. The third layer of skins is the subcutaneous layer. From Figure 1, the outside layer of the skin is the epidermis. The dermis lies beneath the epidermis. The subcutaneous layer lies beneath the dermis. Therefore, choice B is correct.

## RESEARCH SUMMARY PASSAGES
### WHAT TO EXPECT IN THE RESEARCH SUMMARY PASSAGES

In the research summary passages, details regarding an experiment and the data from that experiment are provided. Students need to understand, analyze, and interpret graphs and tables.

Copyright © Mometrix Media. You have been licensed one copy of this document for personal use only. Any other reproduction or redistribution is strictly prohibited. All rights reserved.

Students need understand the design of the experiment and interpret the results of the experiment. Students may be asked to make predictions or inferences or to extrapolate. When reading about the experiment, ask these questions. What is being tested? Why is it being tested? What are the variables? What factors stay the same? Identify the independent variable and the dependent variable. Try to determine the relationship between these variables. Does one factor increase as another factor increases? Does one factor decrease as another factor decreases? Does one factor increase as another factor decreases? Be prepared to interpret data points and extrapolate data from tables and graphs. Remember, many of the questions can be answered by interpreting the charts and graphs without even reading the passage. When studying the graphs and charts, be sure to read all captions, keys, and labels. Identify the axes and the units.

## EXAMPLE

*Partial Passage and Experiment*: Students studied how altitude affects wind speed. Altitude is the distance from the surface of the Earth at sea level. Anemometers were placed at 1 meter, 2 meters, 3 meters, and 4 meters above the ground. Students counted the number of turns each anemometer turned in one minute. Students repeated the test the next two days. That data was also recorded in Table 1.

**Table 1 Anemometer: Turns per Minute**

| Height from Ground <br> Testing Day | 1 meter | 2 meters | 3 meters | 4 meters |
|---|---|---|---|---|
| Day 1 | 14 | 15 | 16 | 17 |
| Day 2 | 16 | 17 | 18 | 19 |
| Day 3 | 13 | 14 | 15 | 16 |

*Question:* **From the data in Table 1, what is the effect of altitude on wind speed?**
   a.   As altitude increases, wind speed remains the same.
   b.   As altitude increases, wind speed decreases.
   c.   As altitude increases, wind speed increases.
   d.   As altitude increases, wind speed increases and then decreases.

*Suggested Approach:* According to Table 1, as altitude increases, wind speed increases. This can be determined by scanning from left to right across any of the three days. The number of turns in each row increases as height from the ground increases. Therefore, choice C is correct.

## CONFLICTING VIEWPOINT PASSAGE
### WHAT TO EXPECT IN THE CONFLICTING VIEWPOINT PASSAGE

In the conflicting viewpoint passages, two or more viewpoints or opinions are presented regarding an observed phenomenon, scientific topic, or scientific concern. Students are expected to evaluate alternative theories, hypotheses, and viewpoints. Students need to compare the viewpoints and recognize and understand the similarities and differences between the viewpoints. Some questions will cover specific details about the viewpoint. Students might be asked to make inferences or draw reasonable conclusions from the information that is provided. Only one of these types of passages is on this test.

Copyright © Mometrix Media. You have been licensed one copy of this document for personal use only. Any other reproduction or redistribution is strictly prohibited. All rights reserved.

## APPROACH FOR THE CONFLICTING VIEWPOINT PASSAGE

1. **It doesn't matter who's right!** When reading the opposing or conflicting viewpoints, stick to the facts in the passage. Don't worry about who you think is right or wrong.
2. **Ignore your own opinion!** Your viewpoint doesn't matter. Just read the passage and get the information needed to answer the questions.
3. **Take shorthand notes.** Jot down or underline the information that supports each viewpoint. Jot down or circle key points of each viewpoint. Only use information that is stated in the viewpoints.
4. **Look for similarities and differences.** Ask yourself how the conflicting viewpoints argue about the same concept or explain the same concept.

## EXAMPLE

*Partial Passage:* After going down the plastic slide at recess, Justin notices that his hair is standing on end. Justin asks his friends Olivia and Sophia why his hair is standing up.

*Olivia's Viewpoint:* Justin picked up electric charges when going down the slide. The electric charges traveled to the ends of his hair. Since like charges repel each other, the individual strands of his hair moved apart from each other, making his hair appear to stand on end.

*Sophia's Viewpoint:* Justin's hair did not pick up electric charges when going down the slide. His hair is standing on end due to some chemical his hair picked up while going down the slide. The chemical made his hair sticky, and that's why his hair is standing on end. Even if Justin's hair did pick up electric charges, like charges attract each other. Electric charges cannot possibly be the reason Justin's hair is standing on end.

**Question: Another student claimed that Justin's hair picked up electrons while going down the slide. Since electrons all have negative charges, the electrons in Justin's hair repelled each other, causing Justin's hair to stand up. Which of the other students would agree this is a possibility?**

   a.  Olivia only
   b.  Sophia only
   c.  Both Olivia and Sophia
   d.  Neither Olivia nor Sophia

*Suggested Approach:* Since negative charges are electric charges, Olivia would agree that Justin's hair may have picked up electrons. Since Sophia specifically stated that Justin's hair did not pick up electric charges, she would not agree that his hair picked up negative charges. Therefore, choice A is correct.

## EXAMPLE

*Partial Passage:* After going down the plastic slide at recess, Justin notices that his hair is standing on end. Justin asks why his hair is standing up. *Olivia's Viewpoint:* Justin picked up electric charges when going down the slide. Since like charges repel each other, the individual strands of his hair moved apart from each other. *Sophia's Viewpoint:* Justin's hair did not pick up electric charges when going down the slide. His hair is standing on end due to some chemical his hair picked up while going down the slide. The chemical made his hair sticky.

Copyright © Mometrix Media. You have been licensed one copy of this document for personal use only. Any other reproduction or redistribution is strictly prohibited. All rights reserved.

**Question:** One student claimed another student spilled a juice box on the slide. Based on the passage, does this support Sophia's viewpoint?

a. Yes; Sophia stated that Justin's hair picked up juice as he went down the slide.
b. Yes; Sophia stated that Justin's hair picked up a chemical. This chemical could have been juice from the juice box.
c. No; Sophia stated that Justin's hair picked up electric charges, not chemicals.
d. No; Sophia stated Justin's hair did not pick up any chemicals.

*Suggested Approach:* Sophia said that Justin's hair picked up chemicals that made his hair sticky. Since juice can be sticky, this claim supports Sophia's viewpoint. Therefore, choice B is correct

Copyright © Mometrix Media. You have been licensed one copy of this document for personal use only. Any other reproduction or redistribution is strictly prohibited. All rights reserved.

# Practice Test

## Practice Questions

*Use the following information for Questions 1-6*

Passage 1

A magnet pulls on objects made of iron or other specific metals. All metals are not pulled by a magnet. These iron objects do not need to actually touch the magnet. The magnet has a magnetic field that is shown by the field lines in Figure 1. The actual field lines are invisible, but small pieces of iron called iron filings line up in paths resembling the field lines when sprinkled near the magnet. The magnetic field lines follow the path shown by the arrows. The south pole of the magnet is marked with the S. The north pole of the magnet is marked with the N.

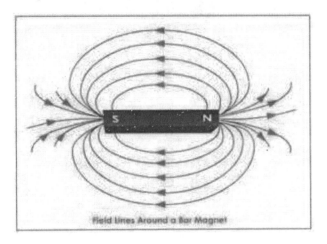

Figure 1

**1. Which of the following best describes the direction of the field lines around the bar magnet shown in Figure 1?**
- a. The field lines move away from the south pole.
- b. The field lines move away from the north pole.
- c. The field lines move back and forth from the north pole.
- d. The field lines move straight away from the magnet in every direction.

**2. Which of the following is true about the poles of the bar magnet in Figure 1?**
- a. The bar magnet has two south poles located at opposite ends of the magnet.
- b. The bar magnet has one south pole and one north pole located near the middle of the bar magnet.
- c. The bar magnet has one south pole and one north pole located at opposite ends of the magnet.
- d. The bar magnet has two north poles located at opposite ends of the magnet.

97

Copyright © Mometrix Media. You have been licensed one copy of this document for personal use only. Any other reproduction or redistribution is strictly prohibited. All rights reserved.

**3. Which of the following best describes the pattern of tiny iron filings sprinkled near a bar magnet?**

    a.  Loops drawn from the north pole to the south pole
    b.  Straight lines drawn towards the magnet from every direction
    c.  Circles drawn around the magnet but not touching the magnet
    d.  Waves drawn back and forth between the north and south pole

**4. Which of the following objects would most likely be attracted to a magnet?**

    a.  A brass button
    b.  A plastic paperclip
    c.  A glass marble
    d.  An iron needle

Passage 2

When two magnets are placed near each other the field lines around each magnet are affected by the field lines of the other magnet. Small iron filings dropped between the two magnets line up with these field lines as shown in Figure 2.

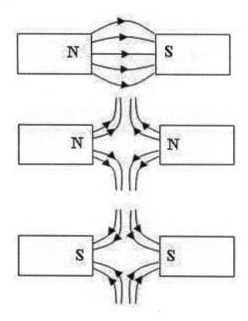

Figure 2

**5. Which of the following best describes the direction of the magnetic field lines between the north pole of one bar magnet and the south pole of another bar magnet?**

    a.  From the north pole of one magnet to the south pole of the other magnet
    b.  From the south pole of one magnet to the north pole of the other magnet
    c.  Away from the north poles of both magnets
    d.  Away from the south poles of both magnets

Copyright © Mometrix Media. You have been licensed one copy of this document for personal use only. Any other reproduction or redistribution is strictly prohibited. All rights reserved.

**6. In which of the cases in Figure 2 do the magnetic field lines move away from both of the poles of the bar magnets shown?**

    a.   When the north pole of one magnet is placed near the north pole of another magnet
    b.   When the north pole of one magnet is placed near the south pole of another magnet
    c.   When the south pole of one magnet is placed near the south pole of another magnet
    d.   When the south pole of one magnet is placed near the north pole of another magnet

*Use the following information for Questions 7-12*

After going down the plastic slide at recess, Justin notices that his hair is standing on end. Justin asks his friends Olivia and Sophia why his hair is standing up.

*Olivia's Viewpoint*

Justin picked up electric charges when going down the slide. The electric charges traveled to the ends of his hair. Since like charges repel each other, the individual strands of his hair moved apart from each other making his hair appear to stand on end.

*Sophia's Viewpoint*

Justin's hair did not pick up electric charges when going down the slide. His hair is standing on end due to some chemical his hair picked up while going doing the slide. The chemical made his hair sticky, and that's why his hair is standing on end. Even if Justin's hair did pick up electric charges, like charges attract each other. Electric charges cannot possibly be the reason Justin's hair is standing on end.

**7. According to the passage, which of the students, if either, would agree that Justin's hair picked up electric charges when Justin went down the slide?**

    a.   Olivia only
    b.   Sophia only
    c.   Both Olivia and Sophia
    d.   Neither Olivia nor Sophia

**8. Another student claimed that Justin's hair picked up electrons while going down the slide. Since electrons all have negative charges, the electrons in Justin's hair repelled each other, causing Justin's hair to stand up. Which of the other students would agree this is a possibility?**

    a.   Olivia only
    b.   Sophia only
    c.   Both Olivia and Sophia
    d.   Neither Olivia nor Sophia

**9. One student claimed another student spilled a juice box on the slide. Based on the passage, does this support Sophia's viewpoint?**

    a.   Yes; Sophia stated that Justin's hair picked up juice as he went down the slide.
    b.   Yes; Sophia stated that Justin's hair picked up a chemical. This chemical could have been juice from the juice box.
    c.   No; Sophia stated that Justin's hair picked up electric charges, not chemicals.
    d.   No; Sophia stated that Justin's hair did not pick up any chemicals.

Copyright © Mometrix Media. You have been licensed one copy of this document for personal use only. Any other reproduction or redistribution is strictly prohibited. All rights reserved.

**10. According to the passage, which of the following statements is true?**

    a. According to Olivia, like charges attract each other.
    b. According to Olivia, like charges repel each other.
    c. According to Sophia, like charges repel each other.
    d. According to Sophia, electrons repel each other.

**11. According to the passage, which of the students would agree that two positive charges have no effect on each other?**

    a. Olivia only
    b. Sophia only
    c. Both Olivia and Sophia
    d. Neither Olivia nor Sophia

**12. According to the passage, which of the following statements does not support Sophia's viewpoint?**

    a. Justin's hair picked up chemicals.
    b. Chemicals are sticky.
    c. Electric charges are sticky.
    d. Justin's hair was sticky.

*Questions 13-18*

*Passage 1*

A food web shows the feeding relationships in an ecosystem. The ecosystem contains a group of organisms called a community. A food web is made up of many food chains. A food chain represents the transfer of energy through a series of organisms in the community. The food chain starts with a producer. Producers include green plants that make their own food by photosynthesis. Primary consumers feed on producers. Primary consumers are herbivores. Herbivores are animals that eat only plants. Secondary consumers feed on primary consumers. Secondary consumers are carnivores or omnivores. Carnivores eat other animals. Omnivores eat plants and other animals. Some food chains have tertiary or quaternary consumers. Tertiary consumers eat secondary

Copyright © Mometrix Media. You have been licensed one copy of this document for personal use only. Any other reproduction or redistribution is strictly prohibited. All rights reserved.

consumers. Quaternary consumers eat tertiary consumers. Figure 1 includes two separate food chains.

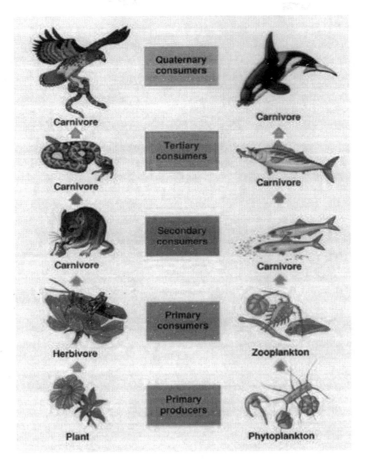

Figure 1

### 13. Which of the following steps in a food chain includes the herbivores?

a. Secondary consumers
b. Quaternary consumers
c. Producers
d. Primary consumers

### 14. According to Figure 1, quaternary consumers would be classified as which of the following?

a. Producers
b. Herbivores
c. Carnivores
d. Zooplankton

### 15. Which of the following organisms is a producer?

a. Snake
b. Phytoplankton
c. Whale
d. Fish

Copyright © Mometrix Media. You have been licensed one copy of this document for personal use only. Any other reproduction or redistribution is strictly prohibited. All rights reserved.

Passage 2

Each step of a food chain represents a trophic level. Food webs usually have four trophic levels. Producers form the first trophic level. Primary consumers form the second trophic level. Secondary consumers form the third trophic level. Tertiary consumers form the fourth trophic level. Some food webs include quaternary consumers. Quaternary consumers form the fifth trophic level. Food webs also contain decomposers and detritivores, which break down dead, decaying plant and animal matter. This organic matter helps nourish the soil. Figure 2 shows a typical food web.

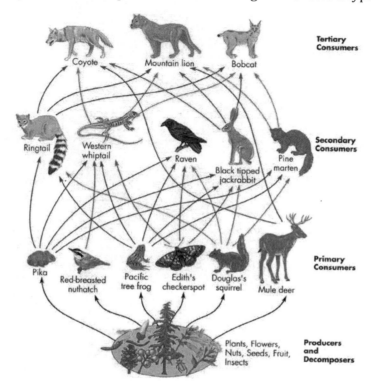

Figure 2

**16. According to this food web, which of the following is not a secondary consumer?**
- a. Bobcat
- b. Western whiptail
- c. Pine marten
- d. Raven

**17. To which trophic level do the producers belong?**
- a. Second
- b. First
- c. Fourth
- d. Third

**18. Which of the following statements is not true concerning food webs?**
- a. Plants belong in the first trophic level.
- b. Herbivores form the second trophic level.
- c. Tertiary consumers form the fourth trophic level.
- d. Secondary consumers form the second trophic level.

Copyright © Mometrix Media. You have been licensed one copy of this document for personal use only. Any other reproduction or redistribution is strictly prohibited. All rights reserved.

*Questions 19-24*

*Passage*

Plants require sunlight, water, and proper nutrients to grow. One necessary plant food nutrient is nitrogen. Plants use nitrogen to build proteins and nucleic acids. Nitrogen gives plants their healthy green color. Nitrogen makes up about 78 percent of the atmosphere, but plants cannot use this type of nitrogen. Nitrogen can form special substances or compounds called nitrates that plants can use. Nitrates are provided to the soil through the nitrogen cycle. Farmers and gardeners can add more nitrogen to the soil by adding fertilizer to the soil. It is important to give the plants the amount of fertilizer recommended by the manufacturer of the fertilizer. If a plant is given too much fertilizer, the plant may die. Plants absorb fertilizer through their roots by osmosis. Water in the soil moves into the roots, carrying the fertilizer along with it. If too much fertilizer is added to the soil, water will move in the opposite direction from the roots to the soil. This harms the plant by causing it to actually lose water rather than take in water.

*Experiment*

Students filled 12 small pots with equal amounts of soil and planted radish seeds in each pot according to the package directions. The pots were divided into four groups. Group A plants were the control group and were watered with regular water. Group B plants were watered with a nitrogen fertilizer solution that was less concentrated than the manufacturer's recommendation. Group C plants were watered with a nitrogen fertilizer solution prepared according to the manufacturer's recommendation. Group D plants were watered with a nitrogen fertilizer solution that was more concentrated than the manufacturer's recommendation. The heights of all plants were measured on the fourteenth day and recorded in Table 1. The average height was calculated for each group. See Figure 2.

**Table 1 Radish Plant Height (cm)**

|         | Group A | Group B | Group C | Group D |
|---------|---------|---------|---------|---------|
| Plant 1 | 47.8    | 51.8    | 54.2    | 51.9    |
| Plant 2 | 47.6    | 51.9    | 54.6    | 52.1    |
| Plant 3 | 48.1    | 52.0    | 54.9    | 51.7    |

Copyright © Mometrix Media. You have been licensed one copy of this document for personal use only. Any other reproduction or redistribution is strictly prohibited. All rights reserved.

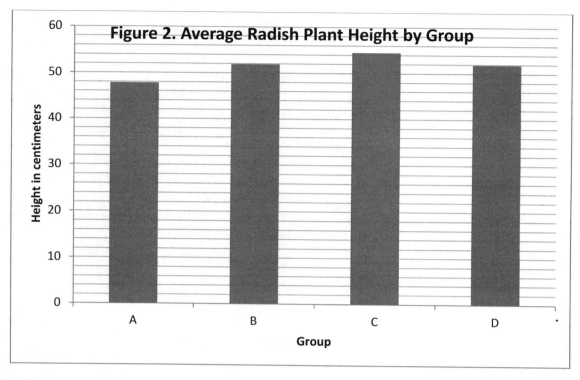

Figure 2. Average Radish Plant Height by Group

**19. Which gas makes up approximately 78 percent of the atmosphere?**

    a. Oxygen
    b. Water vapor
    c. Carbon dioxide
    d. Nitrogen

**20. What was the average height of radish plants for group B?**

    a. 51 cm
    b. 50 cm
    c. 52 cm
    d. 53 cm

**21. What was the tallest radish plant in group A?**

    a. 54.9 cm
    b. 48.1 cm
    c. 48 cm
    d. 55 cm

**22. How do organisms use nitrogen?**

    a. Nitrogen makes up about 78 percent of the atmosphere.
    b. Fertilizer is absorbed through the roots.
    c. Nitrogen is used to form proteins.
    d. Farmers add nitrogen by applying fertilizer.

Copyright © Mometrix Media. You have been licensed one copy of this document for personal use only. Any other reproduction or redistribution is strictly prohibited. All rights reserved.

23. **Which group of plants grew the highest on average?**
    a. Group A
    b. Group B
    c. Group C
    d. Group D

24. **Which of the following statements is true?**
    a. Plants grow best when given more fertilizer than the manufacturer's recommended amount of fertilizer.
    b. Plants grow best when given less fertilizer than the manufacturer's recommended amount of fertilizer.
    c. Plants grow best without any fertilizer.
    d. Plants grow best when given the manufacturer's recommended amount of fertilizer.

*Questions 25-29*

*Passage*

Soils are made up of particles. The spaces between the particles are called pore spaces. The amount of total pore spaces in the soil determines how much water the soil can hold. Porosity is the fraction of the pore space to the total amount of soil. Porosity is usually expressed as a percentage. Soil particles are of different types such as sand, silt, and clay. Sand is coarse and feels gritty. Sand has the largest particle size. Since the particles do not fit together tightly, sand has the largest pore spaces. Sand drains water well. Silt particles are smaller than sand particles but larger than clay particles. Silt feels soft and smooth. Clay has very fine particles that are very tightly packed and very small pore spaces. Clay feels sticky. Clay retains water well. When it rains, some water runs off into rivers and streams, but some water seeps into the soil through the pore spaces. A large amount of water is retained in the soil. This is known as water retention. The two factors that affect the movement of water through the soil are permeability and porosity. Porosity is determined by the volume of the pore spaces compared to the total volume of the soil. Porosity determines the amount of water the soil can hold. Permeability describes how fast the water moves through the soil. Permeability is affected by porosity. See Figure 1.

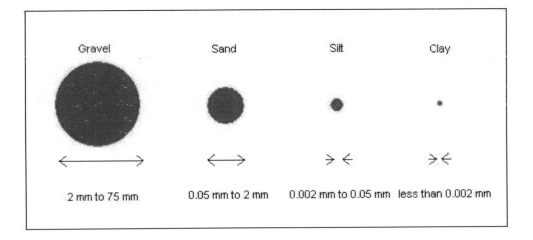

Figure 1

Copyright © Mometrix Media. You have been licensed one copy of this document for personal use only. Any other reproduction or redistribution is strictly prohibited. All rights reserved.

### 25. Which type of material has the smallest particles?

 a. Sand
 b. Silt
 c. Gravel
 d. Clay

### 26. Which description best fits silt?

 a. Large particles and feels sticky
 b. Very small particles and feels coarse
 c. Small particles and feels smooth
 d. Very large particles and feels soft

### 27. Which of the following is correctly defined as how quickly water moves through a soil?

 a. Permeability
 b. Porosity
 c. Water retention
 d. Soil type

*Study 1*

Students designed an experiment to determine the water retention of sand, silt, and clay. Retention is measured by the amount of water remaining in the soil after it has been drained. Students gathered three identical plastic pots with holes in the bottom. Students filled each pot with one of each of the three soil types and weighed the pots. These initial weights were recorded in Table 1. The pots were placed over plastic containers, and 200 ml of water was poured into each pot. Water drained from the pots into the plastic containers. After four hours, the pots were weighed. This data was recorded in Table 1.

**Table 1 Water Retention in Soil**

| Soil Type | Initial Weight (grams) | Final Weight (grams) | Difference in Weight (grams) |
|---|---|---|---|
| Sand | 1,236 | 1,245 | 9 |
| Silt | 1,067 | 1,188 | 121 |
| Clay | 1,040 | 1,222 | 182 |

### 28. What did the pot of silt weigh initially?

 a. 1,236 grams
 b. 1,067 grams
 c. 1,188 grams
 d. 1,040 grams

### 29. Which pot of soil retained the most water?

 a. The pot of sand retained the most water.
 b. The pot of silt retained the most water.
 c. The pot of clay retained the most water.
 d. The pots all retained the same amount of water.

Copyright © Mometrix Media. You have been licensed one copy of this document for personal use only. Any other reproduction or redistribution is strictly prohibited. All rights reserved.

**30. How much water was added initially to each pot?**

   a. 250 ml
   b. 200 ml
   c. 100 ml
   d. 500 ml

*Questions 31-36*

*Passage*

Wind is movement of air. Wind is produced when the surface of the Earth is heated unevenly by the sun. Different regions of land and water absorb the sun's energy differently. The air above warm areas heats up and rises. The air above cool areas cools down and sinks. Rising and sinking air causes low and high pressure regions to form near the Earth and up higher above the ground. Air moves from regions of high pressure toward regions of low pressure. This air movement is wind. Winds are described by speed and direction. Wind speed can be measured by an instrument called an anemometer. Anemometers have cups on the ends of rotating arms. The cups catch the wind, and the anemometer spins. The greater the wind speed, the faster the anemometer turns. Wind direction can be measure by a weather vane. Wind speed has visible effects on land. See Figure 1. Visible effects such as leaves rustling or trees swaying can be seen with the eye.

| Wind speed (mph) | Effects Visible on land |
|---|---|
| Under 1 | Calm: smoke rises vertically |
| 1-3 | Smoke drift indicates wind direction; vanes do not move |
| 4-7 | Wind felt on face; leaves rustle; vanes begin to move |
| 8-12 | Leaves and small twigs are constantly moving; light flags extend |
| 13-18 | Dust, leaves and loose paper is lifted up; small branches move. |
| 19-24 | Small trees begin to sway |
| 25-31 | Large branches of trees in motion; whistling heard in wires |
| 32-38 | Whole trees in motion; resistance felt in walking against wind |
| 39-54 | Twigs and small branches broken off trees |

Figure 1

**31. Which of the following statements is true?**

   a. Warm air rises, and cool air sinks.
   b. Warm air rises, and cool air rises.
   c. Warm air sinks, and cool air rises.
   d. Warm air sinks, and cool air sinks.

**32. Which property of air is measured by an anemometer?**

   a. Temperature
   b. Wind speed
   c. Wind direction
   d. Pressure

Copyright © Mometrix Media. You have been licensed one copy of this document for personal use only. Any other reproduction or redistribution is strictly prohibited. All rights reserved.

**33. According to Table 1, what visible effects can be expected with wind speeds of 10 mph?**

a.  Small branches move.
b.  Small trees begin to sway.
c.  Light flags sway.
d.  Small branches are broken off trees.

*Study*

Students studied how altitude affects wind speed. Altitude is the distance from the surface of the Earth at sea level. Anemometers were placed at 1 meter, 2 meters, 3 meters, and 4 meters above the ground on a high hill with no buildings or trees nearby. Students counted the number of turns each anemometer turned in one minute. The data was recorded in Table 1. Students repeated the test the next two days. That data was also recorded in Table 1.

**Table 1 Anemometer: Turns per Minute**

| Height from ground / Testing Day | 1 meter | 2 meters | 3 meters | 4 meters |
|---|---|---|---|---|
| Day 1 | 14 | 15 | 16 | 17 |
| Day 2 | 16 | 17 | 18 | 19 |
| Day 3 | 13 | 14 | 15 | 16 |

**34. Which of the following is true concerning this study?**

a.  Students studied the effect of altitude on wind speed.
b.  Students studied the effect of temperature on wind speed.
c.  Students studied the effect of temperature on wind direction.
d.  Students studied the effect of altitude on wind direction.

**35. What was the number of turns recorded at 2 meters on Day 3?**

a.  16
b.  17
c.  15
d.  14

**36. From the data in Table 1, what is the effect of altitude on wind speed?**

a.  As altitude increases, wind speed remains the same.
b.  As altitude increases, wind speed decreases.
c.  As altitude increases, wind speed increases.
d.  As altitude increases, wind speed increases and then decreases.

Copyright © Mometrix Media. You have been licensed one copy of this document for personal use only. Any other reproduction or redistribution is strictly prohibited. All rights reserved.

# Answers and Explanations

**1. B:** According to Figure 1, the arrows on the field lines connected to the north pole are pointing away from the north pole. The arrows on the field lines connected to the south pole are pointing towards the south pole. Therefore, choice B is correct.

**2. C:** According to Figure 1, the left end of this bar magnet is marked with an *S*, which indicates a south pole. The right end of the magnet is marked with an *N*, which indicates a north pole. This magnet has one south pole and one north pole located at opposite ends of the magnet. Therefore, choice C is correct.

**3. A:** Iron filings line up with the magnetic field lines. In Figure 1, the field lines form loops from the north pole to the south pole. Therefore, choice A is correct.

**4. D:** The passage states that iron is attracted to magnets, but gives no other information about which other metals are attracted to magnets. Therefore, choice D is correct.

**5. A:** The top two magnets in Figure 2 shows the magnets arranged with the north pole of one magnet near the south pole of another bar magnet. The field lines are draw from the north pole of the magnet on the left toward the south pole of the magnet of the right. Therefore, choice A is correct.

**6. A:** The middle set of magnets in Figure 2 show the field lines being drawn away from both north poles when the north pole of one magnet is placed near the north pole of another magnet. Therefore, choice A is correct.

**7. A:** Sophia's viewpoint states that Justin's hair did not pick up electric charges. Only Olivia stated that Justin's hair picked up electric charges. Therefore, choice A is correct.

**8. A:** Since negative charges are electric charges, Olivia would agree that Justin's hair may have picked up electrons. Therefore, choice A is correct.

**9. B:** Sophia stated that Justin's hair picked up chemicals that made his hair sticky. Since juice can be sticky, this claim supports Sophia's viewpoint. Therefore, choice B is correct.

**10. B:** Only Olivia stated that like charges repel each other. Sophia stated that like charges attract each other. Therefore, choice B is correct.

**11. D:** Olivia stated that like charges repel each other. Sophia stated that like charges attract each other. Neither student states that like charges have no effect on each other. Therefore, choice D is correct.

**12. A:** Sophia said that Justin's hair picked up chemicals that made his hair sticky. Since juice can be sticky, this claim supports Sophia's viewpoint. Therefore, choice B is correct

**13. D:** According to the passage, herbivores are animals that eat only plants. Since primary producers eat plants, primary producers are herbivores. Therefore, choice D is correct.

**14. C:** According to Figure 1, quaternary consumers are labeled carnivores. Therefore, choice C is correct.

**15. B:** According to figure 1, phytoplankton is a producer. Therefore, choice B is correct.

Copyright © Mometrix Media. You have been licensed one copy of this document for personal use only. Any other reproduction or redistribution is strictly prohibited. All rights reserved.

**16. A:** According to Figure 2, the raven, pine marten, and western whiptail are secondary consumers. The bobcat is s tertiary consumer. Therefore, choice A is correct.

**17. B:** According to the passage, producers form the first trophic level, and the food web shows the producers on the lowest level. Therefore, choice B is correct.

**18. D:** According to the passage and Figure 2, secondary consumers form the third trophic level, not the fourth. Therefore, choice D is correct.

**19. D:** According to the passage, nitrogen makes up approximately 78 percent of the Earth's atmosphere. Therefore, choice D is correct.

**20. C:** According to Figure 2, the radish plants in group B grew to an average height of 52 cm. This is determined by the number of divisions between 50 and 60 on the vertical axis. Since there are five divisions between 50 and 60 cm, each division represents 2 cm. Therefore, choice C is correct.

**21. B:** Table 1 lists the individual heights of each plant. The heights of the plants in group A were 47.8 cm, 47.6 cm, and 48.1 cm. The tallest plant in group A was 48.1 cm. Therefore, choice B is correct.

**22. C:** The passage states that plants use nitrogen to form proteins and nucleic acids. While all of the statements in the choices are true, only choice C answers the question that was asked. Therefore, choice C is correct.

**23. C:** According to Figure 2, the plants in group C grew the highest. This is determined by comparing the heights of the bars for each group. Since the bar for group C is the tallest, the plants in group C grew the highest. Therefore, choice C is correct.

**24. D:** According to the passage, it is important to give the plants the amount of fertilizer recommended by the manufacturer of the fertilizer. According to Figure 2, group C, which was given the amount of fertilizer recommended by the manufacturer, grew the highest. Therefore, choice D is correct.

**25. D:** According to the passage, clay has the smallest particles. This can also be seen in Figure 1. Therefore, choice D is correct.

**26. C:** According to the passage, silt is small and feels smooth and soft. According to Figure 1, silt is small, not large. Therefore, choice C is correct.

**27. A:** According to the passage, permeability describes how fast the water moves through the soil. Therefore, choice A is correct.

**28. B:** According to the second column of Table 1, the initial weight of the pot of silt was 1,067 grams. Therefore, choice B is correct.

**29. C:** According to Table 1, the pot of clay had the greatest difference in weight after the water was added. This means the pot of clay retained or held the most water. Therefore, choice C is correct.

**30. B:** According to the passage, students poured 200 ml of water into each pot. Therefore, choice b is correct.

Copyright © Mometrix Media. You have been licensed one copy of this document for personal use only. Any other reproduction or redistribution is strictly prohibited. All rights reserved.

**31. A:** According to the passage, the air above warm areas heats up and rises. The air above cool areas cools down and sinks. This means warm air rises and cool air sinks. Therefore, choice A is correct.

**32. B:** According to the passage, wind speed can be measured by an anemometer. Therefore, choice B is correct.

**33. C:** According to Table 1, when wind speeds are 8-12 mph, leaves and small twigs are constantly moving, and light flags sway. Therefore, choice C is correct.

**34. A:** According to the information given in the passage, students studied how altitude affects wind speed. Therefore, choice A is correct.

**35. D:** According to Table 1, the number of turns at 2 meters on Day 3 was 14. This can be found by scanning down to Day 3 and then over to the 2 meter column. Therefore, choice D is correct.

**36. C:** According to Table 1, as altitude increases, wind speed increases. This can be determined by scanning from left to right across any of the three days. The number of turns in each row increases as height from the ground increases. Therefore, choice C is correct.

Copyright © Mometrix Media. You have been licensed one copy of this document for personal use only. Any other reproduction or redistribution is strictly prohibited. All rights reserved.

# How to Overcome Test Anxiety

Just the thought of taking a test is enough to make most people a little nervous. A test is an important event that can have a long-term impact on your future, so it's important to take it seriously and it's natural to feel anxious about performing well. But just because anxiety is normal, that doesn't mean that it's helpful in test taking, or that you should simply accept it as part of your life. Anxiety can have a variety of effects. These effects can be mild, like making you feel slightly nervous, or severe, like blocking your ability to focus or remember even a simple detail.

If you experience test anxiety—whether severe or mild—it's important to know how to beat it. To discover this, first you need to understand what causes test anxiety.

## Causes of Test Anxiety

While we often think of anxiety as an uncontrollable emotional state, it can actually be caused by simple, practical things. One of the most common causes of test anxiety is that a person does not feel adequately prepared for their test. This feeling can be the result of many different issues such as poor study habits or lack of organization, but the most common culprit is time management. Starting to study too late, failing to organize your study time to cover all of the material, or being distracted while you study will mean that you're not well prepared for the test. This may lead to cramming the night before, which will cause you to be physically and mentally exhausted for the test. Poor time management also contributes to feelings of stress, fear, and hopelessness as you realize you are not well prepared but don't know what to do about it.

Other times, test anxiety is not related to your preparation for the test but comes from unresolved fear. This may be a past failure on a test, or poor performance on tests in general. It may come from comparing yourself to others who seem to be performing better or from the stress of living up to expectations. Anxiety may be driven by fears of the future—how failure on this test would affect your educational and career goals. These fears are often completely irrational, but they can still negatively impact your test performance.

> **Review Video: 3 Reasons You Have Test Anxiety**
> Visit mometrix.com/academy and enter code: 428468

112

Copyright © Mometrix Media. You have been licensed one copy of this document for personal use only. Any other reproduction or redistribution is strictly prohibited. All rights reserved.

# Elements of Test Anxiety

As mentioned earlier, test anxiety is considered to be an emotional state, but it has physical and mental components as well. Sometimes you may not even realize that you are suffering from test anxiety until you notice the physical symptoms. These can include trembling hands, rapid heartbeat, sweating, nausea, and tense muscles. Extreme anxiety may lead to fainting or vomiting. Obviously, any of these symptoms can have a negative impact on testing. It is important to recognize them as soon as they begin to occur so that you can address the problem before it damages your performance.

> **Review Video: 3 Ways to Tell You Have Test Anxiety**
> Visit mometrix.com/academy and enter code: 927847

The mental components of test anxiety include trouble focusing and inability to remember learned information. During a test, your mind is on high alert, which can help you recall information and stay focused for an extended period of time. However, anxiety interferes with your mind's natural processes, causing you to blank out, even on the questions you know well. The strain of testing during anxiety makes it difficult to stay focused, especially on a test that may take several hours. Extreme anxiety can take a huge mental toll, making it difficult not only to recall test information but even to understand the test questions or pull your thoughts together.

> **Review Video: How Test Anxiety Affects Memory**
> Visit mometrix.com/academy and enter code: 609003

# Effects of Test Anxiety

Test anxiety is like a disease—if left untreated, it will get progressively worse. Anxiety leads to poor performance, and this reinforces the feelings of fear and failure, which in turn lead to poor performances on subsequent tests. It can grow from a mild nervousness to a crippling condition. If allowed to progress, test anxiety can have a big impact on your schooling, and consequently on your future.

Test anxiety can spread to other parts of your life. Anxiety on tests can become anxiety in any stressful situation, and blanking on a test can turn into panicking in a job situation. But fortunately, you don't have to let anxiety rule your testing and determine your grades. There are a number of relatively simple steps you can take to move past anxiety and function normally on a test and in the rest of life.

> **Review Video: How Test Anxiety Impacts Your Grades**
> Visit mometrix.com/academy and enter code: 939819

Copyright © Mometrix Media. You have been licensed one copy of this document for personal use only. Any other reproduction or redistribution is strictly prohibited. All rights reserved.

# Physical Steps for Beating Test Anxiety

While test anxiety is a serious problem, the good news is that it can be overcome. It doesn't have to control your ability to think and remember information. While it may take time, you can begin taking steps today to beat anxiety.

Just as your first hint that you may be struggling with anxiety comes from the physical symptoms, the first step to treating it is also physical. Rest is crucial for having a clear, strong mind. If you are tired, it is much easier to give in to anxiety. But if you establish good sleep habits, your body and mind will be ready to perform optimally, without the strain of exhaustion. Additionally, sleeping well helps you to retain information better, so you're more likely to recall the answers when you see the test questions.

Getting good sleep means more than going to bed on time. It's important to allow your brain time to relax. Take study breaks from time to time so it doesn't get overworked, and don't study right before bed. Take time to rest your mind before trying to rest your body, or you may find it difficult to fall asleep.

> **Review Video: The Importance of Sleep for Your Brain**
> Visit mometrix.com/academy and enter code: 319338

Along with sleep, other aspects of physical health are important in preparing for a test. Good nutrition is vital for good brain function. Sugary foods and drinks may give a burst of energy but this burst is followed by a crash, both physically and emotionally. Instead, fuel your body with protein and vitamin-rich foods.

Also, drink plenty of water. Dehydration can lead to headaches and exhaustion, especially if your brain is already under stress from the rigors of the test. Particularly if your test is a long one, drink water during the breaks. And if possible, take an energy-boosting snack to eat between sections.

> **Review Video: How Diet Can Affect your Mood**
> Visit mometrix.com/academy and enter code: 624317

Along with sleep and diet, a third important part of physical health is exercise. Maintaining a steady workout schedule is helpful, but even taking 5-minute study breaks to walk can help get your blood pumping faster and clear your head. Exercise also releases endorphins, which contribute to a positive feeling and can help combat test anxiety.

When you nurture your physical health, you are also contributing to your mental health. If your body is healthy, your mind is much more likely to be healthy as well. So take time to rest, nourish your body with healthy food and water, and get moving as much as possible. Taking these physical steps will make you stronger and more able to take the mental steps necessary to overcome test anxiety.

> **Review Video: How to Stay Healthy and Prevent Test Anxiety**
> Visit mometrix.com/academy and enter code: 877894

Copyright © Mometrix Media. You have been licensed one copy of this document for personal use only. Any other reproduction or redistribution is strictly prohibited. All rights reserved.

# Mental Steps for Beating Test Anxiety

Working on the mental side of test anxiety can be more challenging, but as with the physical side, there are clear steps you can take to overcome it. As mentioned earlier, test anxiety often stems from lack of preparation, so the obvious solution is to prepare for the test. Effective studying may be the most important weapon you have for beating test anxiety, but you can and should employ several other mental tools to combat fear.

First, boost your confidence by reminding yourself of past success—tests or projects that you aced. If you're putting as much effort into preparing for this test as you did for those, there's no reason you should expect to fail here. Work hard to prepare; then trust your preparation.

Second, surround yourself with encouraging people. It can be helpful to find a study group, but be sure that the people you're around will encourage a positive attitude. If you spend time with others who are anxious or cynical, this will only contribute to your own anxiety. Look for others who are motivated to study hard from a desire to succeed, not from a fear of failure.

Third, reward yourself. A test is physically and mentally tiring, even without anxiety, and it can be helpful to have something to look forward to. Plan an activity following the test, regardless of the outcome, such as going to a movie or getting ice cream.

When you are taking the test, if you find yourself beginning to feel anxious, remind yourself that you know the material. Visualize successfully completing the test. Then take a few deep, relaxing breaths and return to it. Work through the questions carefully but with confidence, knowing that you are capable of succeeding.

Developing a healthy mental approach to test taking will also aid in other areas of life. Test anxiety affects more than just the actual test—it can be damaging to your mental health and even contribute to depression. It's important to beat test anxiety before it becomes a problem for more than testing.

> **Review Video: Test Anxiety and Depression**
> Visit mometrix.com/academy and enter code: 904704

Copyright © Mometrix Media. You have been licensed one copy of this document for personal use only. Any other reproduction or redistribution is strictly prohibited. All rights reserved.

# Study Strategy

Being prepared for the test is necessary to combat anxiety, but what does being prepared look like? You may study for hours on end and still not feel prepared. What you need is a strategy for test prep. The next few pages outline our recommended steps to help you plan out and conquer the challenge of preparation.

## STEP 1: SCOPE OUT THE TEST

Learn everything you can about the format (multiple choice, essay, etc.) and what will be on the test. Gather any study materials, course outlines, or sample exams that may be available. Not only will this help you to prepare, but knowing what to expect can help to alleviate test anxiety.

## STEP 2: MAP OUT THE MATERIAL

Look through the textbook or study guide and make note of how many chapters or sections it has. Then divide these over the time you have. For example, if a book has 15 chapters and you have five days to study, you need to cover three chapters each day. Even better, if you have the time, leave an extra day at the end for overall review after you have gone through the material in depth.

If time is limited, you may need to prioritize the material. Look through it and make note of which sections you think you already have a good grasp on, and which need review. While you are studying, skim quickly through the familiar sections and take more time on the challenging parts. Write out your plan so you don't get lost as you go. Having a written plan also helps you feel more in control of the study, so anxiety is less likely to arise from feeling overwhelmed at the amount to cover.

## STEP 3: GATHER YOUR TOOLS

Decide what study method works best for you. Do you prefer to highlight in the book as you study and then go back over the highlighted portions? Or do you type out notes of the important information? Or is it helpful to make flashcards that you can carry with you? Assemble the pens, index cards, highlighters, post-it notes, and any other materials you may need so you won't be distracted by getting up to find things while you study.

If you're having a hard time retaining the information or organizing your notes, experiment with different methods. For example, try color-coding by subject with colored pens, highlighters, or post-it notes. If you learn better by hearing, try recording yourself reading your notes so you can listen while in the car, working out, or simply sitting at your desk. Ask a friend to quiz you from your flashcards, or try teaching someone the material to solidify it in your mind.

## STEP 4: CREATE YOUR ENVIRONMENT

It's important to avoid distractions while you study. This includes both the obvious distractions like visitors and the subtle distractions like an uncomfortable chair (or a too-comfortable couch that makes you want to fall asleep). Set up the best study environment possible: good lighting and a comfortable work area. If background music helps you focus, you may want to turn it on, but otherwise keep the room quiet. If you are using a computer to take notes, be sure you don't have any other windows open, especially applications like social media, games, or anything else that could distract you. Silence your phone and turn off notifications. Be sure to keep water close by so you stay hydrated while you study (but avoid unhealthy drinks and snacks).

Also, take into account the best time of day to study. Are you freshest first thing in the morning? Try to set aside some time then to work through the material. Is your mind clearer in the afternoon or evening? Schedule your study session then. Another method is to study at the same time of day that

Copyright © Mometrix Media. You have been licensed one copy of this document for personal use only. Any other reproduction or redistribution is strictly prohibited. All rights reserved.

you will take the test, so that your brain gets used to working on the material at that time and will be ready to focus at test time.

## STEP 5: STUDY!

Once you have done all the study preparation, it's time to settle into the actual studying. Sit down, take a few moments to settle your mind so you can focus, and begin to follow your study plan. Don't give in to distractions or let yourself procrastinate. This is your time to prepare so you'll be ready to fearlessly approach the test. Make the most of the time and stay focused.

Of course, you don't want to burn out. If you study too long you may find that you're not retaining the information very well. Take regular study breaks. For example, taking five minutes out of every hour to walk briskly, breathing deeply and swinging your arms, can help your mind stay fresh.

As you get to the end of each chapter or section, it's a good idea to do a quick review. Remind yourself of what you learned and work on any difficult parts. When you feel that you've mastered the material, move on to the next part. At the end of your study session, briefly skim through your notes again.

But while review is helpful, cramming last minute is NOT. If at all possible, work ahead so that you won't need to fit all your study into the last day. Cramming overloads your brain with more information than it can process and retain, and your tired mind may struggle to recall even previously learned information when it is overwhelmed with last-minute study. Also, the urgent nature of cramming and the stress placed on your brain contribute to anxiety. You'll be more likely to go to the test feeling unprepared and having trouble thinking clearly.

So don't cram, and don't stay up late before the test, even just to review your notes at a leisurely pace. Your brain needs rest more than it needs to go over the information again. In fact, plan to finish your studies by noon or early afternoon the day before the test. Give your brain the rest of the day to relax or focus on other things, and get a good night's sleep. Then you will be fresh for the test and better able to recall what you've studied.

## STEP 6: TAKE A PRACTICE TEST

Many courses offer sample tests, either online or in the study materials. This is an excellent resource to check whether you have mastered the material, as well as to prepare for the test format and environment.

Check the test format ahead of time: the number of questions, the type (multiple choice, free response, etc.), and the time limit. Then create a plan for working through them. For example, if you have 30 minutes to take a 60-question test, your limit is 30 seconds per question. Spend less time on the questions you know well so that you can take more time on the difficult ones.

If you have time to take several practice tests, take the first one open book, with no time limit. Work through the questions at your own pace and make sure you fully understand them. Gradually work up to taking a test under test conditions: sit at a desk with all study materials put away and set a timer. Pace yourself to make sure you finish the test with time to spare and go back to check your answers if you have time.

After each test, check your answers. On the questions you missed, be sure you understand why you missed them. Did you misread the question (tests can use tricky wording)? Did you forget the information? Or was it something you hadn't learned? Go back and study any shaky areas that the practice tests reveal.

Copyright © Mometrix Media. You have been licensed one copy of this document for personal use only. Any other reproduction or redistribution is strictly prohibited. All rights reserved.

Taking these tests not only helps with your grade, but also aids in combating test anxiety. If you're already used to the test conditions, you're less likely to worry about it, and working through tests until you're scoring well gives you a confidence boost. Go through the practice tests until you feel comfortable, and then you can go into the test knowing that you're ready for it.

## Test Tips

On test day, you should be confident, knowing that you've prepared well and are ready to answer the questions. But aside from preparation, there are several test day strategies you can employ to maximize your performance.

First, as stated before, get a good night's sleep the night before the test (and for several nights before that, if possible). Go into the test with a fresh, alert mind rather than staying up late to study.

Try not to change too much about your normal routine on the day of the test. It's important to eat a nutritious breakfast, but if you normally don't eat breakfast at all, consider eating just a protein bar. If you're a coffee drinker, go ahead and have your normal coffee. Just make sure you time it so that the caffeine doesn't wear off right in the middle of your test. Avoid sugary beverages, and drink enough water to stay hydrated but not so much that you need a restroom break 10 minutes into the test. If your test isn't first thing in the morning, consider going for a walk or doing a light workout before the test to get your blood flowing.

Allow yourself enough time to get ready, and leave for the test with plenty of time to spare so you won't have the anxiety of scrambling to arrive in time. Another reason to be early is to select a good seat. It's helpful to sit away from doors and windows, which can be distracting. Find a good seat, get out your supplies, and settle your mind before the test begins.

When the test begins, start by going over the instructions carefully, even if you already know what to expect. Make sure you avoid any careless mistakes by following the directions.

Then begin working through the questions, pacing yourself as you've practiced. If you're not sure on an answer, don't spend too much time on it, and don't let it shake your confidence. Either skip it and come back later, or eliminate as many wrong answers as possible and guess among the remaining ones. Don't dwell on these questions as you continue—put them out of your mind and focus on what lies ahead.

Be sure to read all of the answer choices, even if you're sure the first one is the right answer. Sometimes you'll find a better one if you keep reading. But don't second-guess yourself if you do immediately know the answer. Your gut instinct is usually right. Don't let test anxiety rob you of the information you know.

If you have time at the end of the test (and if the test format allows), go back and review your answers. Be cautious about changing any, since your first instinct tends to be correct, but make sure you didn't misread any of the questions or accidentally mark the wrong answer choice. Look over any you skipped and make an educated guess.

At the end, leave the test feeling confident. You've done your best, so don't waste time worrying about your performance or wishing you could change anything. Instead, celebrate the successful

Copyright © Mometrix Media. You have been licensed one copy of this document for personal use only. Any other reproduction or redistribution is strictly prohibited. All rights reserved.

completion of this test. And finally, use this test to learn how to deal with anxiety even better next time.

> **Review Video: 5 Tips to Beat Test Anxiety**
> Visit mometrix.com/academy and enter code: 570656

## Important Qualification

Not all anxiety is created equal. If your test anxiety is causing major issues in your life beyond the classroom or testing center, or if you are experiencing troubling physical symptoms related to your anxiety, it may be a sign of a serious physiological or psychological condition. If this sounds like your situation, we strongly encourage you to seek professional help.

Copyright © Mometrix Media. You have been licensed one copy of this document for personal use only. Any other reproduction or redistribution is strictly prohibited. All rights reserved.

# How to Overcome Your Fear of Math

The word *math* is enough to strike fear into most hearts. How many of us have memories of sitting through confusing lectures, wrestling over mind-numbing homework, or taking tests that still seem incomprehensible even after hours of study? Years after graduation, many still shudder at these memories.

The fact is, math is not just a classroom subject. It has real-world implications that you face every day, whether you realize it or not. This may be balancing your monthly budget, deciding how many supplies to buy for a project, or simply splitting a meal check with friends. The idea of daily confrontations with math can be so paralyzing that some develop a condition known as *math anxiety*.

But you do NOT need to be paralyzed by this anxiety! In fact, while you may have thought all your life that you're not good at math, or that your brain isn't wired to understand it, the truth is that you may have been conditioned to think this way. From your earliest school days, the way you were taught affected the way you viewed different subjects. And the way math has been taught has changed.

Several decades ago, there was a shift in American math classrooms. The focus changed from traditional problem-solving to a conceptual view of topics, de-emphasizing the importance of learning the basics and building on them. The solid foundation necessary for math progression and confidence was undermined. Math became more of a vague concept than a concrete idea. Today, it is common to think of math, not as a straightforward system, but as a mysterious, complicated method that can't be fully understood unless you're a genius.

This is why you may still have nightmares about being called on to answer a difficult problem in front of the class. Math anxiety is a very real, though unnecessary, fear.

Math anxiety may begin with a single class period. Let's say you missed a day in 6th grade math and never quite understood the concept that was taught while you were gone. Since math is cumulative, with each new concept building on past ones, this could very well affect the rest of your math career. Without that one day's knowledge, it will be difficult to understand any other concepts that link to it. Rather than realizing that you're just missing one key piece, you may begin to believe that you're simply not capable of understanding math.

This belief can change the way you approach other classes, career options, and everyday life experiences, if you become anxious at the thought that math might be required. A student who loves science may choose a different path of study upon realizing that multiple math classes will be required for a degree. An aspiring medical student may hesitate at the thought of going through the necessary math classes. For some this anxiety escalates into a more extreme state known as *math phobia*.

Math anxiety is challenging to address because it is rooted deeply and may come from a variety of causes: an embarrassing moment in class, a teacher who did not explain concepts well and contributed to a shaky foundation, or a failed test that contributed to the belief of math failure.

These causes add up over time, encouraged by society's popular view that math is hard and unpleasant. Eventually a person comes to firmly believe that he or she is simply bad at math. This belief makes it difficult to grasp new concepts or even remember old ones. Homework and test

Copyright © Mometrix Media. You have been licensed one copy of this document for personal use only. Any other reproduction or redistribution is strictly prohibited. All rights reserved.

grades begin to slip, which only confirms the belief. The poor performance is not due to lack of ability but is caused by math anxiety.

Math anxiety is an emotional issue, not a lack of intelligence. But when it becomes deeply rooted, it can become more than just an emotional problem. Physical symptoms appear. Blood pressure may rise and heartbeat may quicken at the sight of a math problem – or even the thought of math! This fear leads to a mental block. When someone with math anxiety is asked to perform a calculation, even a basic problem can seem overwhelming and impossible. The emotional and physical response to the thought of math prevents the brain from working through it logically.

The more this happens, the more a person's confidence drops, and the more math anxiety is generated. This vicious cycle must be broken!

The first step in breaking the cycle is to go back to very beginning and make sure you really understand the basics of how math works and why it works. It is not enough to memorize rules for multiplication and division. If you don't know WHY these rules work, your foundation will be shaky and you will be at risk of developing a phobia. Understanding mathematical concepts not only promotes confidence and security, but allows you to build on this understanding for new concepts. Additionally, you can solve unfamiliar problems using familiar concepts and processes.

Why is it that students in other countries regularly outperform American students in math? The answer likely boils down to a couple of things: the foundation of mathematical conceptual understanding and societal perception. While students in the US are not expected to *like* or *get* math, in many other nations, students are expected not only to understand math but also to excel at it.

Changing the American view of math that leads to math anxiety is a monumental task. It requires changing the training of teachers nationwide, from kindergarten through high school, so that they learn to teach the *why* behind math and to combat the wrong math views that students may develop. It also involves changing the stigma associated with math, so that it is no longer viewed as unpleasant and incomprehensible. While these are necessary changes, they are challenging and will take time. But in the meantime, math anxiety is not irreversible—it can be faced and defeated, one person at a time.

## False Beliefs

One reason math anxiety has taken such hold is that several false beliefs have been created and shared until they became widely accepted. Some of these unhelpful beliefs include the following:

***There is only one way to solve a math problem***. In the same way that you can choose from different driving routes and still arrive at the same house, you can solve a math problem using different methods and still find the correct answer. A person who understands the reasoning behind math calculations may be able to look at an unfamiliar concept and find the right answer, just by applying logic to the knowledge they already have. This approach may be different than what is taught in the classroom, but it is still valid. Unfortunately, even many teachers view math as a subject where the best course of action is to memorize the rule or process for each problem rather than as a place for students to exercise logic and creativity in finding a solution.

***Many people don't have a mind for math***. A person who has struggled due to poor teaching or math anxiety may falsely believe that he or she doesn't have the mental capacity to grasp

Copyright © Mometrix Media. You have been licensed one copy of this document for personal use only. Any other reproduction or redistribution is strictly prohibited. All rights reserved.

mathematical concepts. Most of the time, this is false. Many people find that when they are relieved of their math anxiety, they have more than enough brainpower to understand math.

**Men are naturally better at math than women**. Even though research has shown this to be false, many young women still avoid math careers and classes because of their belief that their math abilities are inferior. Many girls have come to believe that math is a male skill and have given up trying to understand or enjoy it.

**Counting aids are bad**. Something like counting on your fingers or drawing out a problem to visualize it may be frowned on as childish or a crutch, but these devices can help you get a tangible understanding of a problem or a concept.

Sadly, many students buy into these ideologies at an early age. A young girl who enjoys math class may be conditioned to think that she doesn't actually have the brain for it because math is for boys, and may turn her energies to other pursuits, permanently closing the door on a wide range of opportunities. A child who finds the right answer but doesn't follow the teacher's method may believe that he is doing it wrong and isn't good at math. A student who never had a problem with math before may have a poor teacher and become confused, yet believe that the problem is because she doesn't have a mathematical mind.

Students who have bought into these erroneous beliefs quickly begin to add their own anxieties, adapting them to their own personal situations:

**I'll never use this in real life**. A huge number of people wrongly believe that math is irrelevant outside the classroom. By adopting this mindset, they are handicapping themselves for a life in a mathematical world, as well as limiting their career choices. When they are inevitably faced with real-world math, they are conditioning themselves to respond with anxiety.

**I'm not quick enough**. While timed tests and quizzes, or even simply comparing yourself with other students in the class, can lead to this belief, speed is not an indicator of skill level. A person can work very slowly yet understand at a deep level.

**If I can understand it, it's too easy**. People with a low view of their own abilities tend to think that if they are able to grasp a concept, it must be simple. They cannot accept the idea that they are capable of understanding math. This belief will make it harder to learn, no matter how intelligent they are.

**I just can't learn this**. An overwhelming number of people think this, from young children to adults, and much of the time it is simply not true. But this mindset can turn into a self-fulfilling prophecy that keeps you from exercising and growing your math ability.

The good news is, each of these myths can be debunked. For most people, they are based on emotion and psychology, NOT on actual ability! It will take time, effort, and the desire to change, but change is possible. Even if you have spent years thinking that you don't have the capability to understand math, it is not too late to uncover your true ability and find relief from the anxiety that surrounds math.

Copyright © Mometrix Media. You have been licensed one copy of this document for personal use only. Any other reproduction or redistribution is strictly prohibited. All rights reserved.

# Math Strategies

It is important to have a plan of attack to combat math anxiety. There are many useful strategies for pinpointing the fears or myths and eradicating them:

***Go back to the basics***. For most people, math anxiety stems from a poor foundation. You may think that you have a complete understanding of addition and subtraction, or even decimals and percentages, but make absolutely sure. Learning math is different from learning other subjects. For example, when you learn history, you study various time periods and places and events. It may be important to memorize dates or find out about the lives of famous people. When you move from US history to world history, there will be some overlap, but a large amount of the information will be new. Mathematical concepts, on the other hand, are very closely linked and highly dependent on each other. It's like climbing a ladder – if a rung is missing from your understanding, it may be difficult or impossible for you to climb any higher, no matter how hard you try. So go back and make sure your math foundation is strong. This may mean taking a remedial math course, going to a tutor to work through the shaky concepts, or just going through your old homework to make sure you really understand it.

***Speak the language***. Math has a large vocabulary of terms and phrases unique to working problems. Sometimes these are completely new terms, and sometimes they are common words, but are used differently in a math setting. If you can't speak the language, it will be very difficult to get a thorough understanding of the concepts. It's common for students to think that they don't understand math when they simply don't understand the vocabulary. The good news is that this is fairly easy to fix. Brushing up on any terms you aren't quite sure of can help bring the rest of the concepts into focus.

***Check your anxiety level***. When you think about math, do you feel nervous or uncomfortable? Do you struggle with feelings of inadequacy, even on concepts that you know you've already learned? It's important to understand your specific math anxieties, and what triggers them. When you catch yourself falling back on a false belief, mentally replace it with the truth. Don't let yourself believe that you can't learn, or that struggling with a concept means you'll never understand it. Instead, remind yourself of how much you've already learned and dwell on that past success. Visualize grasping the new concept, linking it to your old knowledge, and moving on to the next challenge. Also, learn how to manage anxiety when it arises. There are many techniques for coping with the irrational fears that rise to the surface when you enter the math classroom. This may include controlled breathing, replacing negative thoughts with positive ones, or visualizing success. Anxiety interferes with your ability to concentrate and absorb information, which in turn contributes to greater anxiety. If you can learn how to regain control of your thinking, you will be better able to pay attention, make progress, and succeed!

***Don't go it alone***. Like any deeply ingrained belief, math anxiety is not easy to eradicate. And there is no need for you to wrestle through it on your own. It will take time, and many people find that speaking with a counselor or psychiatrist helps. They can help you develop strategies for responding to anxiety and overcoming old ideas. Additionally, it can be very helpful to take a short course or seek out a math tutor to help you find and fix the missing rungs on your ladder and make sure that you're ready to progress to the next level. You can also find a number of math aids online: courses that will teach you mental devices for figuring out problems, how to get the most out of your math classes, etc.

***Check your math attitude***. No matter how much you want to learn and overcome your anxiety, you'll have trouble if you still have a negative attitude toward math. If you think it's too hard, or just

Copyright © Mometrix Media. You have been licensed one copy of this document for personal use only. Any other reproduction or redistribution is strictly prohibited. All rights reserved.

have general feelings of dread about math, it will be hard to learn and to break through the anxiety. Work on cultivating a positive math attitude. Remind yourself that math is not just a hurdle to be cleared, but a valuable asset. When you view math with a positive attitude, you'll be much more likely to understand and even enjoy it. This is something you must do for yourself. You may find it helpful to visit with a counselor. Your tutor, friends, and family may cheer you on in your endeavors. But your greatest asset is yourself. You are inside your own mind – tell yourself what you need to hear. Relive past victories. Remind yourself that you are capable of understanding math. Root out any false beliefs that linger and replace them with positive truths. Even if it doesn't feel true at first, it will begin to affect your thinking and pave the way for a positive, anxiety-free mindset.

Aside from these general strategies, there are a number of specific practical things you can do to begin your journey toward overcoming math anxiety. Something as simple as learning a new note-taking strategy can change the way you approach math and give you more confidence and understanding. New study techniques can also make a huge difference.

Math anxiety leads to bad habits. If it causes you to be afraid of answering a question in class, you may gravitate toward the back row. You may be embarrassed to ask for help. And you may procrastinate on assignments, which leads to rushing through them at the last moment when it's too late to get a better understanding. It's important to identify your negative behaviors and replace them with positive ones:

*Prepare ahead of time*. Read the lesson before you go to class. Being exposed to the topics that will be covered in class ahead of time, even if you don't understand them perfectly, is extremely helpful in increasing what you retain from the lecture. Do your homework and, if you're still shaky, go over some extra problems. The key to a solid understanding of math is practice.

*Sit front and center*. When you can easily see and hear, you'll understand more, and you'll avoid the distractions of other students if no one is in front of you. Plus, you're more likely to be sitting with students who are positive and engaged, rather than others with math anxiety. Let their positive math attitude rub off on you.

*Ask questions in class and out*. If you don't understand something, just ask. If you need a more in-depth explanation, the teacher may need to work with you outside of class, but often it's a simple concept you don't quite understand, and a single question may clear it up. If you wait, you may not be able to follow the rest of the day's lesson. For extra help, most professors have office hours outside of class when you can go over concepts one-on-one to clear up any uncertainties. Additionally, there may be a *math lab* or study session you can attend for homework help. Take advantage of this.

*Review*. Even if you feel that you've fully mastered a concept, review it periodically to reinforce it. Going over an old lesson has several benefits: solidifying your understanding, giving you a confidence boost, and even giving some new insights into material that you're currently learning! Don't let yourself get rusty. That can lead to problems with learning later concepts.

Copyright © Mometrix Media. You have been licensed one copy of this document for personal use only. Any other reproduction or redistribution is strictly prohibited. All rights reserved.

# Teaching Tips

While the math student's mindset is the most crucial to overcoming math anxiety, it is also important for others to adjust their math attitudes. Teachers and parents have an enormous influence on how students relate to math. They can either contribute to math confidence or math anxiety.

As a parent or teacher, it is very important to convey a positive math attitude. Retelling horror stories of your own bad experience with math will contribute to a new generation of math anxiety. Even if you don't share your experiences, others will be able to sense your fears and may begin to believe them.

Even a careless comment can have a big impact, so watch for phrases like *He's not good at math* or *I never liked math*. You are a crucial role model, and your children or students will unconsciously adopt your mindset. Give them a positive example to follow. Rather than teaching them to fear the math world before they even know it, teach them about all its potential and excitement.

Work to present math as an integral, beautiful, and understandable part of life. Encourage creativity in solving problems. Watch for false beliefs and dispel them. Cross the lines between subjects: integrate history, English, and music with math. Show students how math is used every day, and how the entire world is based on mathematical principles, from the pull of gravity to the shape of seashells. Instead of letting students see math as a necessary evil, direct them to view it as an imaginative, beautiful art form – an art form that they are capable of mastering and using.

Don't give too narrow a view of math. It is more than just numbers. Yes, working problems and learning formulas is a large part of classroom math. But don't let the teaching stop there. Teach students about the everyday implications of math. Show them how nature works according to the laws of mathematics, and take them outside to make discoveries of their own. Expose them to math-related careers by inviting visiting speakers, asking students to do research and presentations, and learning students' interests and aptitudes on a personal level.

Demonstrate the importance of math. Many people see math as nothing more than a required stepping stone to their degree, a nuisance with no real usefulness. Teach students that algebra is used every day in managing their bank accounts, in following recipes, and in scheduling the day's events. Show them how learning to do geometric proofs helps them to develop logical thinking, an invaluable life skill. Let them see that math surrounds them and is integrally linked to their daily lives: that weather predictions are based on math, that math was used to design cars and other machines, etc. Most of all, give them the tools to use math to enrich their lives.

Make math as tangible as possible. Use visual aids and objects that can be touched. It is much easier to grasp a concept when you can hold it in your hands and manipulate it, rather than just listening to the lecture. Encourage math outside of the classroom. The real world is full of measuring, counting, and calculating, so let students participate in this. Keep your eyes open for numbers and patterns to discuss. Talk about how scores are calculated in sports games and how far apart plants are placed in a garden row for maximum growth. Build the mindset that math is a normal and interesting part of daily life.

Finally, find math resources that help to build a positive math attitude. There are a number of books that show math as fascinating and exciting while teaching important concepts, for example: *The Math Curse; A Wrinkle in Time; The Phantom Tollbooth;* and *Fractals, Googols and Other Mathematical Tales*. You can also find a number of online resources: math puzzles and games,

Copyright © Mometrix Media. You have been licensed one copy of this document for personal use only. Any other reproduction or redistribution is strictly prohibited. All rights reserved.

videos that show math in nature, and communities of math enthusiasts. On a local level, students can compete in a variety of math competitions with other schools or join a math club.

The student who experiences math as exciting and interesting is unlikely to suffer from math anxiety. Going through life without this handicap is an immense advantage and opens many doors that others have closed through their fear.

## Self-Check

Whether you suffer from math anxiety or not, chances are that you have been exposed to some of the false beliefs mentioned above. Now is the time to check yourself for any errors you may have accepted. Do you think you're not wired for math? Or that you don't need to understand it since you're not planning on a math career? Do you think math is just too difficult for the average person?

Find the errors you've taken to heart and replace them with positive thinking. Are you capable of learning math? Yes! Can you control your anxiety? Yes! These errors will resurface from time to time, so be watchful. Don't let others with math anxiety influence you or sway your confidence. If you're having trouble with a concept, find help. Don't let it discourage you!

Create a plan of attack for defeating math anxiety and sharpening your skills. Do some research and decide if it would help you to take a class, get a tutor, or find some online resources to fine-tune your knowledge. Make the effort to get good nutrition, hydration, and sleep so that you are operating at full capacity. Remind yourself daily that you are skilled and that anxiety does not control you. Your mind is capable of so much more than you know. Give it the tools it needs to grow and thrive.

Copyright © Mometrix Media. You have been licensed one copy of this document for personal use only. Any other reproduction or redistribution is strictly prohibited. All rights reserved.

# Thank You

We at Mometrix would like to extend our heartfelt thanks to you, our friend and patron, for allowing us to play a part in your journey. It is a privilege to serve people from all walks of life who are unified in their commitment to building the best future they can for themselves.

The preparation you devote to these important testing milestones may be the most valuable educational opportunity you have for making a real difference in your life. We encourage you to put your heart into it—that feeling of succeeding, overcoming, and yes, conquering will be well worth the hours you've invested.

We want to hear your story, your struggles and your successes, and if you see any opportunities for us to improve our materials so we can help others even more effectively in the future, please share that with us as well. **The team at Mometrix would be absolutely thrilled to hear from you!** So please, send us an email (support@mometrix.com) and let's stay in touch.

Copyright © Mometrix Media. You have been licensed one copy of this document for personal use only. Any other reproduction or redistribution is strictly prohibited. All rights reserved.

# Additional Bonus Material

Due to our efforts to try to keep this book to a manageable length, we've created a link that will give you access to all of your additional bonus material.

Please visit https://www.mometrix.com/bonus948/actaspireg4
to access the information.

Copyright © Mometrix Media. You have been licensed one copy of this document for personal use only. Any other reproduction or redistribution is strictly prohibited. All rights reserved.